a TEEN'S GUIDE
for surviving and thriving in the 21st century

by Michael H. Popkin, PhD
and
Peggy Hendrickson, MA, LMSW, ACSW

Copyright ©2012 by Active Parenting Publishers

All rights reserved. Printed in the United States of America.

No part of this book may be reproduced in any form without written permission of the publisher.

Published by Active Parenting Publishers, Atlanta, Georgia.

ISBN-10:   1-59723-273-4

ISBN-13:   978-1-59723-273-9

TABLE OF CONTENTS

CHAPTER 3
RESPONSIBILITY AND DISCIPLINE

CHAPTER 4
BUILDING COURAGE AND SELF-ESTEEM

CHAPTER 5
DRUGS, SEXUALITY, AND VIOLENCE: REDUCING THE RISKS, PART 1

CHAPTER 6
DRUGS, SEXUALITY, AND VIOLENCE: REDUCING THE RISKS, PART 2

Teens in Action: You're Welcome Here

You're Welcome Here

No matter your faith,
Your country, or race,
If you're willing to learn,
You're welcome here.

Calm and cool
Or playing the fool
If you want to get ahead,
You're welcome here.

Whatever your creed
Or past misdeeds
If you want to improve
You're welcome here.

Straight, gay, or bi
Drop in and say "hi."
We've got your back, and
You're welcome here.

Small town or urban
Country or suburban,
Pull up a chair
Let down your hair
And if you don't have any
You're still welcome here!

- Michael Popkin

welcome!

Welcome to *Teens in Action!* As you begin this six-session journey toward meeting the many challenges of the teen years, you're probably wondering what to expect.

You may be participating in a workshop with your parents as part of a *Families in Action* program, or you may be participating in a "teens-only" group. Or you may just be reading this book by itself. Either way, you'll be learning skills that will help you have better relationships with your parents, family, friends, and teachers—plus you'll increase your chances of having the life you want to have. Not sure what life you want to have? No problem. Develop the skills now, and you will have them when you need them. As Abe Lincoln once said,

> *I will study and make myself ready, and then maybe my chance will come.*

Life is full of opportunities, but if you aren't ready for them, they can pass you by quicker than your final life in a video game.

you'll be challenged.

Life is full of challenges. Sometimes you meet those challenges successfully, and you move on to the next level, as in that video game just mentioned. Sometimes those challenges can block your way, and it becomes one of those costly "learning experiences" that adults are always talking about.

Many of the challenges that teens face are associated with school. After all, going to school is something that almost all teens in our society do, and for at least nine months out of every year, it's where a lot of life happens. But what's so challenging about school? How about some of these for starters:

Adjusting to a New School Building

Chances are that your school building is going to change at some point during your teen years, and probably more than once: elementary to middle school, middle to high school. The new school building may be larger than you're used to, and you'll need to find your way around. Fast! If school means a building change for you, it may also mean that you've moved from being one of the older students in your old school to being one of the younger. That change in status can be an unwelcome shock.

Making New Friends

Every new school year presents opportunities to meet different people, especially when you're going to a new school. Even if you're not, you're bound to see some new faces. Meeting new people and trying to fit in can be stressful, but it's also a great chance to make new friends and try out a different set of students, too.

Class Schedules

Your school probably requires students to move to a new classroom for each period. You'll need to keep track of where you're supposed to be and when.

Many Teachers

Most students have a different teacher for each subject. Some you may love. Others, not so much. They may have different expectations of you in terms of behavior, homework, and effort. Some may be nice, supportive, and even fun. There may be others that you find difficult to deal with. Your challenge is to get along with and learn from ALL of your teachers.

New Rules and Academic Demands

A new school has new rules and new academic demands. You'll probably have more homework than you're used to. You'll need to learn new study skills such as taking notes, organizing your homework, and being responsible for a number of different assignments at one time.

Adolescence

You're also entering a challenging time of your life: adolescence. This is a period of amazing changes: physical, mental, emotional, social, sexual, spiritual—you name it. There's a lot of joy to be had in these years, but few get through it without some suffering. The good news is that life usually gets a whole lot better on the other side of adolescence.

Peer Pressure

The desire to be accepted as a member of a certain group or to be friends with people you admire is a very powerful force, even for adults, but adolescents experience it more than other age groups. It can be a positive force or a negative force, so pick your friends wisely.

your parents will be challenged.

The *Teens in Action* program helps young teens master new skills to successfully meet life's challenges, and one of the big ones is learning how to get along with parents. The challenge of the teen years is also a challenge for parents of teens. Take this Doonesbury cartoon, for example:

Reprinted with permission of UNIVERSAL PRESS SYNDICATE © 1994 G.B. Trudeau. All rights reserved.

What could *possibly* be so challenging for parents of teens? It's important for teens to know this if they hope to get along better with their parents, so check out this list.

Some of the Challenges for Parents

1. **To support their teens' changing needs** Parents need to be able to support their teens while, at the same time, allowing them to take on more responsibility.

2. **To allow their teens freedom within limits** Teens need guidance, but they must also learn to make their own decisions and to accept the consequences of their own actions and behavior.

3. **To be involved in their teens' education** Parents want their teens to be successful in school. They have to figure out how best to provide guidance and support without taking over their teens' responsibilities.

4. **To keep lines of communication open** Teens usually begin spending more time with friends, which leaves less time for family. Parents need to learn how to keep lines of communication open so they can be a source of support and encouragement.

5. **To work themselves out of a job** Parenting is the only job in the world for which the goal is to work yourself OUT of a job. The end result of parenting is to no longer be needed (at least not on a regular basis) So, while all of the above is going on, parents also have to learn how to let go so that their teens can become productive adults.

If you and your parents are taking a *Families in Action* course together or if your parents are taking an *Active Parenting of Teens* course on their own, you're in luck because you're probably going to like a lot of what they're learning to do to help you meet your own challenges.

On the other hand, if you're taking a *Teens in Action* course and your parents are not participating, then you can:

a. Throw a tantrum and maybe punch a hole in the wall. (No, we aren't serious about that one!)

b. See if you can get them a copy of *Active Parenting of Teens Parent's Guide* so they can learn the parenting side of what you're learning.

c. Use what you learn in this course to help make your own life successful, and do what you can to build a positive relationship with them. After all, this is YOUR life we're talking about!

d. Both b and c.

WHAT'S A "TEEN ACTION REPORT"?

At the end of each chapter in this guide, you'll find a Teen Action Report: a list of questions and activities for you to think about and to complete during the week. You may want to keep a journal to write down your thoughts and feelings. You can use the questions in this section as topics for your journal entries. Keeping a journal will help you get more out of the program. For example, here are some questions that you can journal about:

about your school

1. What do you like about your school?

2. What are (or what do you think will be) your greatest challenges in middle or high school?

3. What do you think will be your greatest successes in school?

about yourself

1. What do you like most about being you? Are there things you DON'T like about yourself? Are you comfortable with who you are?

2. What are some of your strengths?

3. What are you looking forward to?

4. What are you fearful about?

about your family

1. What do you like about your family?

2. Why do you need your family?

3. Who are you within your family? Are you a helper? An encourager? A friend?

4. How can you be a better family member?

5. What can you do to help your family be as good as it can be?

6. Read the "Job Description for Teens" and the "Job Description for Parents". How well do you do your job? What would you like to improve?

job descriptions for teens and parents

Both teens and parents have important roles in life. Think of it as though it were a job. A teen or a parent has duties and responsibilities—call it a job description.

EMPLOYMENT OPPORTUNITIES

WANTED: TEENS

Rapidly maturing individuals needed for developing the qualities of a successful adult member of society. Must be willing to explore, to feel, to experience, to play, to learn, to love, and to grow. Should be a team player willing to work with friends, family, teachers and others to achieve success for themselves and for others. Successful candidates will be willing to gradually take on more responsibility for their lives and their futures, learn from their experience (and the experience of others), and strive to reach their full potential.

Salary: Seriously? There may be an allowance if the family can afford it. You may be asked to get a job and contribute to your family instead. There are, however, a ton of benefits.

WANTED: PARENTS

Mature adults willing to accept responsibility for the health, welfare, and safety of their entire family, including themselves. This includes maintaining food, clothing, shelter, health care, and education. Parents are responsible for guiding their teens' growth and development in order for teens to develop courage, cooperation, responsibility, respect, self-esteem, and other qualities of character. Parents will do their best to provide the support and discipline necessary to help their teens mature into successful adults. The successful candidates will see their teens take their places in the adult world as contributing members of society. Parents will partner with their teens and others, in the goal of helping the teen develop to his or her full potential.

Salary: Nada. Not even allowance. However, the benefits, once again, are extraordinary.

If You Are in a *Teens in Action* or *Families in Action* Group...

During the next six sessions, you'll be actively engaged in a fun and exciting group-learning program. The following contains important information about attending weekly sessions.

what to wear

Please wear comfortable, casual clothes that allow for free movement. Tuxedos and formal gowns are strongly discouraged.

when you're feeling ill

Please don't attend sessions if you have a contagious illness like the flu or leprosy. In the event that you can't attend a session, please contact a staff member.

group leaders

Parents' Group Leader (if you're taking the class with parents)

NAME: _____ PHONE: _____

Teens' Group Leader(s)

NAME: _____ PHONE: _____

NAME: _____ PHONE: _____

If you miss a session, please read the next chapter in this *Teen's Guide* so you will be caught up when you come to the next session.

PLEASE don't stop coming to the program just because you have to miss a session. Your Group Leader will be glad to talk with you individually before or after the session to go over the material you may have missed in your absence.

WE HOPE YOU ENJOY THE PROGRAM AND FIND IT PERSONALLY REWARDING. GOOD LUCK TO YOU AND YOUR FAMILY!

what the program can do for you

Family Enrichment

You'll learn skills that will help you resolve conflicts at home and get along better with parents and other family members. If you're participating in a Families in Action Parent & Teen Group, you and your parent(s) will learn new skills together and have the opportunity to practice them together between sessions.

School Success

Students learn people skills, responsibility-taking skills, goal-setting skills, and lots of other skills that help them to experience success in school.

Life Success

Students learn skills to build courage and self-esteem; cooperate with others and work well in groups; communicate effectively with both peers and adults; and (stop me if you've heard this before) lots more. These skills provide the basis for success in all areas of life.

what to expect from your program

1. **Six sessions** The Families in Action and Teens in Action programs each meet for six weeks in a row, for either 2 or 2 1/2 hours each session. A ten-minute break is scheduled in the middle of each session. Refreshments are served. (If refreshments aren't served, I'd complain.)

2. **Program activities** include games, videos, discussion, role-plays, and other activities. If you're participating in a Families in Action Parent & Teen Group, you'll spend part of each session in a teens-only group and part with the teens and parents together.

3. **Teens meet in groups of peers** to learn and discuss skills. Parents meet in their groups to learn more about being effective parents. Parents and students come together to practice skills for family enrichment (parent-teen group only).

4. **Who's this program for?** The Families in Action and Teens in Action programs are especially designed for students who are in or entering junior high or middle school. However, this book can be helpful to students as young as 10 and as old as you still want to learn.

5. **Teen Group Leaders and Parent Group Leaders** are people who care about families with junior high and middle school students. They're specially trained to be your guides in this program. Be nice to them.

6. **Every participant is treated with dignity and respect.** A principle of the Teens in Action and Families in Action programs is that every person is a unique individual worthy of respect.

7. **Your privacy and personal issues will be respected.** While everyone in your group will be given the opportunity to share information about him or herself, no one has to share anything they are uncomfortable sharing. And what's shared in the group should stay in the group!

8. **Ground Rules help group members to feel more comfortable.** One of the tasks of the group during the first session is to develop Ground Rules. See below for a list of some of the Ground Rules that have worked well for other groups.

9. **Between sessions, participants are asked to:**
   - Read the *Teen's Guide* pages for that session;
   - Actively participate in Home Activities; and
   - Complete the Teen Action Report exercises at the end of each chapter.

GROUND RULES

ground rules

1. Everyone is entitled to his or her opinion.

2. Everyone must listen.

3. Put-downs are not allowed.

4. It's OK to say what you feel.

5. Keep private information private.

6. One person talks at a time.

7. _____

8. _____

9. _____

10. _____

CHAPTER 1

TO SURVIVE AND THRIVE

f you're a teenager or plan on becoming one, this book is for you. It's got some great ideas for making your life better right now and a whole lot better later. Now, all of these ideas didn't just come from us—the authors. Like most great ideas, they have evolved over hundreds of years from the work of lots of very smart people. But ideas by themselves don't improve anything. They have to be put into action. Put a great idea into a young person's head and hopefully you will see…

Teens in Action!

This doesn't' mean that you won't take time to think, to feel, to reflect on your options and make thoughtful decisions. We hope you do! In fact, this book will show you some good ways for doing just that. But the result of this process needs to be Action. (Or else you may very well spend your life wishing you had done something you knew you should have, if only you had moved on it.)

We want you to dream your own dreams, develop your own talents, and live the life that is best for you. This book, and the program that goes with it, will help. But (and remember this phrase) it's your life. You get to choose how to live it. Sure, there are rules and limits you have to follow, but ultimately, the life you get is going to be most influenced by the choices you make and the actions you take.

Now, let's get on to ways of seeing YOU in action!

WHY IT'S TOUGH TO BE A TEEN

Most children can hardly wait to becoming teenagers. They look forward to important achievements like learning to drive, getting a job, going out on dates, graduating from high school, and enjoying more independence and freedom.

You, as a teenager, are one of our country's most valuable resources! You have great amounts of energy, enthusiasm, creativity, and idealism. You possess the advantage of having your whole life ahead of you and opportunity to make good decisions about how you will live it. You can take a look around at the mistakes the adult world has made and create a better future for yourself and for the world as a whole. You can ultimately make a real difference and become a force for change.

The teen years are full of possibility, but they're also full of challenges!

Teens face social challenges such as:
Will other people like and accept me?
Will anyone ever ask me out or accept a date with me?
How can I be part of this or that group?
Why do I feel so DIFFERENT from everybody else?

Teens face family challenges like:
How can I deal with living with my parents for another six to ten years?
When will I be allowed to have more freedom?
How can I prove to my family that I'm responsible?
Why do my parents treat me like a baby?
When will my parents get off my back?

Teens face physical challenges such as:
When will my body develop?
Will my skin ever clear up?
Will I ever lose this "baby fat?"
What can I do to look and feel my best?
When will my voice change?

Teens also face academic challenges such as:
How will I measure up at school?
When will I do all this homework?
Will I do well enough in school to get into a good college or get a good job?
What am I going to DO for the rest of my life?

Teens are also sensitive to world issues that affect them, like:
How can we keep the world safe for my future?
Will we ever have world peace?
How can we clean up the earth's environment?
Will I ever be able to make a living? Own a home? Start a family? Find a good job?

Teens face spiritual and ethical challenges such as:
What do I believe? What do I value? What is the nature of my relationship with other people? With the world? With God? What is the purpose of my life?

This book won't answer all of these questions for you, but it will help you develop the skills to meet these challenges for yourself over time. So, to begin, let's have a look at that brain of yours.

this is your brain...on adolescence

Science has uncovered a lot about why the teen years are often so challenging as well as so full of opportunity. For starters, a rapid and intense period of brain growth occurs from age 11 to 14 (slightly earlier in girls than boys). This rapid growth—the largest since infancy!—is followed by a period of pruning that can last all the way to the mid- or late-twenties. The brain connections that are used during that time become coated with a substance called *myelin* and grow stronger, while those that aren't used are pruned back and lost. This pruning occurs from the back of the brain to the front, as shown in the diagram below.

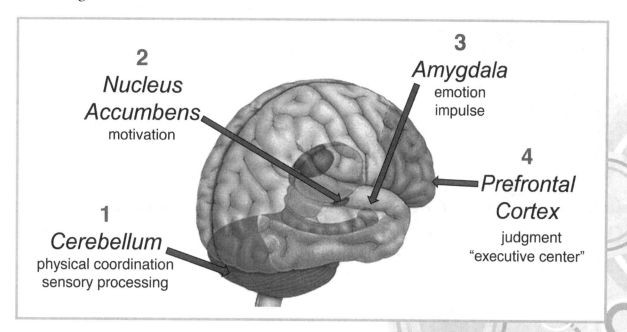

2
Nucleus Accumbens
motivation

3
Amygdala
emotion
impulse

4
Prefrontal Cortex
judgment
"executive center"

1
Cerebellum
physical coordination
sensory processing

It starts with the *cerebellum*, which controls physical coordination and sensory processing.

Then on to the *nucleus accumbens,* which handles motivation…

Next to the *amygdala,* the seat of emotion.

And last, but certainly not least, the *prefrontal cortex,* the executive part of the brain that handles:

- Sound decision making
- Empathy
- Considering consequences
- Regulating emotions
- Self-awareness, and
- Morality

Is anybody you know short on a few of these characteristics? Here's a little secret about adults. We all look back at our teen years and remember a lot of foolish things we did that we wish we hadn't. We now know that at least part of the reason we made these errors in judgment was because during the teen years, the brain (and specifically its executive center) is still "under construction." Of course, knowing this doesn't relieve us of responsibility for our actions, and it won't relieve you, either. But it may help you understand why you still need the support and guidance of parents and other adults throughout the teen years. As these years go by and your brain develops more, you'll need less and less of this support, and eventually you'll become an adult yourself.

SCHOOL SUCCESS

School is the primary responsibility in most teens' lives. Success in school is a starting point for success in life. This doesn't mean that every successful student has a perfect life or even a perfect report card. Nor does it mean that without a college education a person will be miserable. However, many jobs in today's society require special skills, so the need for advanced educational degrees and technical training becomes greater every year.

School success means more than just good grades! There are five major areas of success that are important for teens to think about:

academic success

Good grades aren't everything, but they do matter. Academic success is measured by grades and achievement test scores. It may also be measured by how actively involved a student is in the learning process. So, even if you don't get the best grades, you can achieve academic success by staying engaged and doing your best with your school work. This is good preparation for life beyond school, where being a hard worker often gets us further than being the smartest or the quickest employee in the organization.

social success

This is success in being accepted by a positive peer group. It means knowing how to develop good relationships with others. You can start on the path to social success by finding a group of people with interests similar to your own. Having good communication skills and being encouraging to other people are also helpful.

physical success

This means successfully maintaining your own health and well being. It includes caring enough about yourself (having high self-esteem) that you're willing to put time and energy into being healthy. Physical success means good nutrition, regular exercise, and avoiding unhealthy habits and behavior like smoking cigarettes, using alcohol or other drugs, or becoming sexually active too early.

behavioral success

Behavioral success means that in most situations, whether you're at home, at school, or anywhere else, you're able to make good choices about how you should behave. It means choosing positive ways to achieve your goals. Behavioral success requires good decision-making and problem-solving skills. When a teen succeeds in this area, it shows that he or she is becoming more responsible and independent

psychological success

Psychological success is measured by one's ability to cope with life. It means you're emotionally stable, well integrated into society, and free from harmful addictions. It does not mean you're always happy and never experience ups and downs. All teens go through rocky emotional times and mood swings. Psychological success is more about your emotional state in the long run and your ability to become an emotionally mature adult.

PROFILE OF A SUCCESSFUL STUDENT

If you are participating in a *Teens in Action* or *Families in Action* program, you will be completing the following exercise with your group, but you can also complete it on your own.

In the first column, list some accomplishments that you associate with successful students. These should also be things that *you* would like to accomplish. In the second column, describe the actions a student needs to take to succeed at each accomplishment. Two examples are included. Remember…

Positive action leads to positive consequences!

**A SUCCESSFUL STUDENT
ACCOMPLISHES THESE THINGS:**

BY TAKING THESE ACTIONS:

Gets good grades	➡	Completes homework every day Takes notes during class
Has a lot of friends	➡	Is friendly to everyone Doesn't gossip or spread rumors
	➡	
	➡	
	➡	
	➡	
	➡	

When you THINK positive, FEEL positive, and DO positive things,

SUCCESS IS INEVITABLE!

WHAT'S IN YOUR CHARACTER?

Once upon a time in Sweden...

In 1628 the King of Sweden had his subjects build one of the world's greatest battleships ever, the *Wasa*. What made this ship so great was an upper deck of cannon in addition to the usual first deck. As the day of its launch grew near, the people of Stockholm, from nobles to townspeople, became more and more excited to see the mighty ship set sail. Finally, the day arrived and the *Wasa* took to the seas for its maiden voyage. It hit a storm scarcely a mile out, rolled over, and sank. The problem wasn't so much the storm. Other ships had withstood far worse. The problem was that the *Wasa* didn't have enough weight in its hull, or *ballast*, to counter-balance the heavy upper row of cannon and stabilize itself. Lacking the proper ballast, the *Wasa* was no match for the storm's winds and waves. It simply toppled over and went down like a rock.

Think of yourself as a ship about to set sail on the journey of a lifetime. Like the *Wasa*, you'll likely hit some stormy seas from time to time. What will help you make it through without capsizing? The same thing that would have helped the *Wasa*: ballast. Now we're using the second definition of the word:

> **bal•last**   *noun* /ˈba-lest/
>
> **:** that which gives stability to character

This kind of ballast comes from the core values and qualities of character that you can build to give your life balance and stability when the waves get high and the winds blow hard.

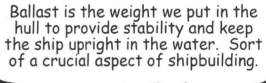

Written by Michael H. Popkin. Art by Ron Wheeler.

TOP 5 QOCs*

There are many qualities of character that can help people survive and thrive in a democratic society, but five form the foundation upon which most other qualities build.

COURAGE: A democratic society provides many opportunities for people to succeed, but success is not guaranteed, nor is it easy to attain. Those with the confidence to take worthwhile risks have the best chance to thrive. And when life gets tough, those with the courage to persevere are more likely to succeed. Among teenagers, it takes a lot of courage to resist peer pressure, to stand up for oneself or for others, and to think independently. From the French word *coeur*, meaning heart, courage is a teen's inner strength. We will focus on ways of instilling this fundamental quality in Chapters 2 and 4.

RESPONSIBILITY: Recognizing our obligations, knowing right from wrong, accepting the consequences of our choices… The trait of responsibility includes all of these. Taking responsibility for our choices creates opportunities for us to learn from our experiences, which helps us to make better decisions in the future. We'll explore the concept of responsibility and how to learn it throughout this book, and especially in Chapter 3.

COOPERATION: A teen who learns to live and work cooperatively with others has a much better chance to succeed than the lone wolf. Competition has its role in our society, but the individual who values teamwork is one who moves society forward. In Chapter 2 we'll discover communication skills that will help you work cooperatively with others while solving problems and making decisions cooperatively.

RESPECT: The concept of mutual respect is a cornerstone of life in any democratic society, particularly one that includes a lot of diversity. When we treat others respectfully and expect them to treat us the same, we make way for the free sharing of ideas that eventually solve problems and create a better society for everyone.

SELF-ESTEEM: Teens who believe they are worthwhile human beings, with talents and dreams that are worthy of respect, have the best chance of thriving. In fact, high self-esteem leads to courage, responsibility, and cooperation. And seeing oneself as someone who embodies these positive qualities builds higher self-esteem. We'll explore this cycle in Chapter 2 as we look at how teens can build self-esteem based on positive attitudes and actions, not self-hype.

By developing these five key qualities in your own character, you'll give yourself the ballast you need to stay steady as you encounter the challenges of your teen years and beyond.

✱ Qualities of Character

RESPECT: IT'S MUTUAL

Teens who grow up in a democratic society such as ours learn from an early age that "all people are created equal under the law." Some teens today are so sensitive to signs of disrespect from others that when they feel someone has "dissed" them, they strike back at the offender with acts of violence, even murder. Reactions like this come from deep discouragement and low self-esteem. But violence in response to disrespect is never justified. The best way to get respect from others is to:

1. Always respect yourself.
2. Always treat others with respect.

This is what we mean by *mutual* respect. You may be thinking, "Easier said than done," and you're right. Respecting yourself and others is not always going to be the easy choice, but it will always be the *best* choice—one that will pay off in positive results. Here are a few pointers to help you get on the right track.

You respect yourself when you:

- Think positive thoughts about yourself and about others.

- Behave so that you give others no reason to think negative thoughts about you (although some people, driven by low self-esteem or discouragement, may still do it).

- Take actions and behave so that you don't risk your health, safety, or good reputation, nor do you risk harming the welfare of others.

- Expect others to treat you with dignity and respect.

For both teens and parents, showing respect for one another ("mutual respect") is one of the most important skills for getting along in a family. Part of this skill is the ability to recognize and avoid *dis*respectful behavior.

SHOWING RESPECT

In the chart below, the left column lists some ways we can be disrespectful to others, and even to ourselves. Finish filling in the right column by writing some ways that we can show respect instead. Then add a few new examples in the blank rows.

WE'RE DISRESPECTFUL TO OTHERS WHEN WE...	WE CAN SHOW THEM RESPECT BY...
Yell or curse at them	
Call them names	
Belittle them	
Use mean-spirited sarcasm	
Don't listen when they speak	

MY CHOICES MATTER!

Q: What's the most powerful tool or weapon known to humans?

A: The power of choice.

Humans are constantly making choices. Through our choices we change ourselves, those around us, and the world itself.

Here's the great thing about choice: Nobody can take it away from you. People and circumstances can limit your choices, but you're always free to choose how you'll respond. You can choose to cooperate or resist; accept responsibility or deny it; choose to act with courage or fear, honesty or deceit, forgiveness or revenge. Through your choices you communicate to the world who you really are and what kind of character you're choosing to develop. Your choices will influence or perhaps even determine what happens to you in your life.

Of course all choices don't carry equal weight. Think about that as you fill in some of your own choices below.

DECISIONS, DECISIONS...

If you are participating in a *Teens in Action* or *Families in Action* program, you may be completing the following exercise in your group, but you can also complete it on your own.

Use your power of choice! Fill in your own answers for the following questions.

If you could choose a movie to watch right now, which would it be?

_____

If you could choose any meal at a restaurant, what would you order?

_____

If you could get together with a friend to do something, what would you do?

_____

If you could visit any place in the world, where would you visit?

_____

If you could master one skill or talent, what would you choose?

_____

If you could make the world a better place, what would you choose to do?

_____

CHALLENGES TEENS FACE TODAY

We said that teens will likely encounter some stormy seas on their voyage into the future. Some of these challenges threaten teens' safety. Others threaten their health. Still others concern things teens do to themselves or obstacles they may need to overcome in order to reach their goals and dreams.

As you think about your life and the community and society in which you live, what do you think are the greatest risks or challenges for teens?

You might think about these in terms of things you're worried about or things you know that other teens are worried about. You might even think about the things you know your parents are concerned about.

The most important challenges teens face today are:

1. _____

2. _____

3. _____

4. _____

5. _____

6. _____

7. _____

8. _____

9. _____

10. _____

drugs, sexuality, and violence: the problem

Many of the challenges that teens face today can be grouped into three broad categories: drugs, sexuality, and violence.

DRUGS, including alcohol and tobacco, pose a serious threat to the health and welfare of teens. Maybe you already know of someone who died from a drug overdose or emphysema caused by smoking tobacco. Maybe you know a victim of a drunk driving accident. If not, you probably will at some point. It's unlikely that you'll get through your teen years without having to make some difficult choices about drugs. In Chapter 5 we'll learn more about chemical dependency and other terrible consequences of drug use.

SEXUAL PRESSURES come from both inside and out. The choices you make in your teen years about sexual involvement will be influenced by pressure other people put on you and by your own desires. Sexual feelings are normal and very much a part of who we are, but before becoming sexually active, teens should be fully aware of the risks. They need strong values concerning sexual behavior, and they need to develop a plan for how they'll cope with sexual pressures. We'll discuss values, assertive communication, and refusal skills in Chapters 5 and 6.

VIOLENCE is a major concern in our society. Bullying, fighting, date violence, and even school shootings have increased the need to address this problem. Like sexual pressures, violence can come from inside or out. On the inside there is anger. Many teens have a lot of it, but they have no clear idea how to express it. In Chapter 4 we'll learn more about the purpose of anger and positive ways of handling it. Some teens live with violence in their homes in the form of child or spouse abuse. Some live in neighborhoods plagued by violent gangs. And we all live in a world where violence is glorified in every kind of media from magazines to movies. We'll discuss various aspects of violence in Chapters 5 and 6, with special focus on gangs and bullying.

getting help

The really good news is that most teens make it through their teen years without experiencing life-threatening problems. But teen pressures and challenges can still seem like an obstacle course. In this guide we'll present skills and new ways of thinking that can help you avoid problems before they begin. We'll be exploring ideas like:

1. **Keeping the lines of communication open between you and your parents or some other trusted adult.** If not your parents, there are many other adults in the community who are specially trained in handling teen stresses: school teachers, school counselors, community/youth workers, social workers, religious leaders, and medical professionals.

2. **Making good choices about whom your close friends are.** It's important to be able to communicate and get along with a variety of people. However, we each have a core group of close, personal friends. If you choose to have friends who have positive values and who usually make good choices for their lives and their behaviors, you'll avoid one of the most difficult teen challenges of all: negative peer pressure.

3. **Choosing to be involved in positive use of leisure time.** There are many ways for teens to use their free time. It's during the hours right after school that teens are most likely to get into trouble. If you have a plan for how to use that time in a constructive and positive way, you'll be less likely to get involved in harmful situations. For example, you can dedicate your afternoon time to school clubs and extracurricular activities, sports, volunteer work, or spiritual youth groups and activities. And, of course, there's always homework. Be sure to leave enough time for that.

4. **Having a plan.** Consider yourself warned: At times, you will be tempted or pressured to—or maybe you even think you *want* to— do something risky, unhealthy, or plain dangerous. That's why it's important to have a plan for how you'll deal with these temptations and pressures when they come along. We'll teach you many skills that will help you develop a plan for making the most of your teen years and beyond.

In spite of our best intentions, human beings do make mistakes. If you realize that you've made an error in judgment, it doesn't mean you're a "bad" person. It does mean that you need some additional support. It's always difficult to make the first call to someone you don't know or to talk about something you've done that you're ashamed of. However, there are people in your community who have chosen their jobs because they want to help people with problems. They're used to hearing about the mistakes people have made. Asking for help when you need it is the right and courageous thing to do.

PEOPLE WHO CAN HELP

Take a few minutes right now to list some of the people that you could turn to if you needed some help or support.

Parents or other close relatives:

Name: _____ Phone: _____ E-mail: _____

Name: _____ Phone: _____ E-mail: _____

Adult neighbor or friend:

Name: _____ Phone: _____ E-mail: _____

Schoolteacher or counselor who I trust:

Name: _____ Phone: _____ E-mail: _____

Religious leader (minister, rabbi, priest, imam, etc.):

Name: _____ Phone: _____ E-mail: _____

Medical person (doctor, nurse, or other):

Name: _____ Phone: _____ E-mail: _____

Community person (youth worker, social worker, counselor, etc.):

Name: _____ Phone: _____ E-mail: _____

Other:

Name: _____ Phone: _____ E-mail: _____

WHAT ABOUT PARENTS?

Good news: Scientists have recently discovered that parents were not, in fact, put on this earth to make your life miserable. On the other hand, neither are they here to make sure your life will be easy and that you'll get everything you want. The truth is that your parents can be one of your most important resources as you move through your teen years… or they can be the people you most "love to hate." If you don't like what's happening between you and your parents, you can do something about it. We'll work on some of the ways that you can build a positive relationship with your parents throughout this book.

In the Introduction we included "job descriptions" for teens and parents. If you haven't already read these, please do so now.

Parents have a very important job to do. It begins when they have their first child and doesn't end until that child is an independent adult. And like any important job, it has a purpose:

The Purpose of Parenting:

To protect and prepare their children and teens
to survive and thrive in the kind of society
in which they will live.

In the seven million years or so that scientists tell us humans have inhabited our planet, this purpose hasn't changed at all. What has changed is "the kind of society in which they will live." As society changes, what it takes to survive and thrive also changes. This also means that parents will need to use different skills for guiding their teens than were used in past generations. Keeping up to date with training is part of any job!

Now, let's take a look at your purpose as an adolescent:

The Purpose of Adolescence:

To protect and prepare ourselves
to survive and thrive in the kind of society
in which we will live.

Sounds familiar doesn't it? Your purpose and your parents' purpose have something incredibly important in common. Both are based on you becoming a thriving member of society. You're teammates whose purpose is to protect you and prepare you to have a good life.

Okay, so you and your parents are on the same team, but as with any team, players have different positions or what we call "roles."

Parent's Role: LEADER

The parent's role has always been to be the leader in the family. Like the president of a company or the principal of a school, the leader is responsible for making final decisions that affect the entire organization.

Teen's Role: LEARNER and active participant

The teen's role is more than that of a learner. Remember that diagram of the executive center of your brain—the one that develops last? Although you're growing and developing, you still have a few years of learning left before you are fully developed and out on your own. During that time, parents are still the leaders in the family, but leaders who should allow you to actively participate in decisions that affect your life.

styles of parenting

Teens may think the best parents are those who let them do anything they want. That may sound like a good idea at first, but if left to their own devices, most teens wouldn't be able to teach themselves all of the skills they'll need to make it on their own in the adult world. They are bound to make lots of painful mistakes before learning life's difficult lessons. Sometimes these mistakes change the rest of a teen's life for the worse, such as when a teen has a baby before she knows how to make a living.

 Some parents are too lenient and don't provide limits to their teen's freedom. We call them *permissive* or "doormat" parents. We can represent this style of parenting with a zigzag.

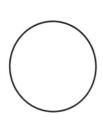 Some parents think the way to be a good parent is to control every move their teen makes. These "dictator" parents who use the *autocratic* approach to parenting may have their teen's best interest in mind, but the unfortunate result is that their teens don't learn how to make their own choices and to accept the outcomes of their choices. We represent this style of parenting with a circle.

 When parents use the *active* style of parenting, they provide their teens with freedom within limits. The diagram for this style of parenting is a circle with a zigzag inside.

This is the method of parenting that we encourage parents to use. In active parenting, parents allow teens to make more and more of their own decisions. As teens earn their parents' trust by being responsible, making good decisions, and using their freedom wisely, they earn more freedom and independence. In this way, teens are able to grow into independent, successful adults.

What can you do to help your parents be successful in using active parenting?

- Respectfully discuss what you want and give good reasons rather than whining or using anger.

- Accept that we all have to learn to live within limits in our society.

- Recognize that your parents have a responsibility to make the final decisions in matters of health, safety, and family values.

- Learn to accept "no" gracefully.

parents are people, too!

It's easy to forget that parents are people, too. They have their hopes and their dreams, their joys and their disappointments just as teens do. Parents have good days when their self-esteem is high and they feel able to meet their responsibilities with ease and grace. Parents also have bad days when just getting through the day is almost more than they can accomplish. Just as teens need personal space and consideration, so do parents.

It's not always easy for teens to think in terms of their parents' needs, but a teen who does can make a major contribution to the harmony of his or her family. Plus, learning to think this way makes it easier to get along with all kinds of people.

Tough Love Labors Lost

William Shakespeare is probably the best-known writer of all time. Although we do not know much about his personal life, we do have reason to believe that he was once a teenager. Like most teens, he probably had his share of conflicts with his parents, who, like most 16th century parents, practiced a form of parenting that was the forerunner of what is now known as "tough love." While we don't advocate this parenting style, we couldn't help wondering what a conversation between a prodigy like Shakespeare and his frustrated, tough-loving father may have sounded like....

William, your grades! Now, I know we've had this conversation before...

Then, as surely as day follows night, we shall have it again.

Are you sassing me?

Doth the bee sass the flower from which his honey pours? Doth the dawn sass the night, or devils, by thy word, give pause to curb their tongues when angels pass?

What does that even mean?

It means, "whatever."

I **HATE** that word. It is positively maddening.

Though this be madness, yet there is method in't.

Written by Michael H. Popkin. Art by Ron Wheeler.

FAMILY ENRICHMENT ACTIVITY: TAKING TIME FOR FUN!

We sometimes forget the fun part of being in a family. Busy schedules don't leave much room for "quality time", and families that are mired in conflict rarely prioritize fun. But fun may be exactly what your family needs! Enjoyable shared activities help to strengthen family relationships, and besides, they're fun! This week, get together with your family and come up with some activities that you'll all enjoy. For example:

- Play a sport, throw a ball around, or shoot baskets.
- Prepare a meal or a fancy dessert together.
- Play a game together.
- Go on an outing: hiking, a museum, a sports event, or a festival.

To get the most out of the activity…

- Choose something that you'll all enjoy.
- Have some suggestions of your own, but also ask your parents for ideas.
- Keep it fun! Don't use the time for confrontation.

Find time to do at least one fun activity with your family this week. Afterwards, write about what you did and how it went in the spaces below.

THE FUN THAT WE HAD

Who participated? _____

What activity did you do? _____

_____

_____

How did it go? _____

_____

_____

_____

HOME ACTIVITIES

If you're participating in a *Teens in Action* or *Families in Action* program, you will be completing some of the exercises and activities in this guide with your group during sessions. Your group leader will assign the ones you didn't get to (as well as some additional skill practice) as Home Activities for you to do between sessions. That list is duplicated here for your convenience.

Regardless of whether you're participating in the program, you'll get more out of this guide when you complete the exercises in each chapter and practice your new skills in real-life situations. So be sure to do your Home Activities for each chapter. Below you'll see what you need to do to make the most of what you learned in Chapter 1.

1. Read Chapters 1 and 2 of this guide.

2. Complete the "Showing Respect" chart on page 29.

3. Answer the questions for the "Decisions, Decisions..." exercise on page 30.

4. Choose a fun activity to do with your parent(s) or your whole family. Afterwards, answer the questions under "The Fun That We Had" on page 41.

5. Answer the "Teen Action Report" questions for Chapter 1 on page 42.

TEEN ACTION REPORT

Write your responses to the following questions on a separate sheet of paper or in a journal.

about yourself

1. What are some of the personal qualities that make you special?

2. What qualities would you like to strengthen in order to become a person you respect and admire?

3. Do you treat other people with respect? How might you be able to be more respectful towards others?

4. What are the most important choices you've made in your life so far? What impact have they had?

about your family

1. Do the members of your family treat each other with mutual respect? If not, what can you do to improve your own behavior and the way you treat your family members?

2. What choices have you helped make in your family? What choices would you LIKE to help make in your family?

3. What do the members of your family enjoy doing together?

about your school

1. What positive qualities of character do you see in your friends? Your teachers?

2. What choices have you made that affect your education? (For example, have you chosen to take certain classes, join a team or a club, or take steps to get accepted to a college or vocational school?)

CHAPTER 2

COOPERATION & COMMUNICATION

Tyra, 15

Tyra, fifteen, had a huge crush on Grant, who was twenty-one. When they started dating, Tyra knew that her mom wouldn't approve, so she kept it a secret. I can handle it, she told herself. I'm mature for my age. Besides, Grant is so sweet, and he says he really likes me. After the two were intimate, Tyra was excited and happy. But when she became pregnant, Grant made himself scarce and wouldn't answer her calls or texts. Tyra knew she had to confess all to her mother. It was going to be the hardest thing she'd ever done.

Raymond, 12

Raymond, twelve, told himself that lots of kids' parents got divorced these days. But when his dad had told him he was moving out, it was like the wind had been knocked out of him. Sure, his parents fought a lot, but they had always assured him that their fighting was no big deal. Now he'd be lucky to see his dad every two weeks. Nothing would be the same again. Suddenly, Raymond hated everything about his life.

Jenny, 17

Jenny, seventeen, was devastated. Being overweight had always bothered her, but she'd managed to live with it. She had friends, and she did well in school. But nothing this bad had ever happened to her before. How could people be so cruel? She'd been online, checking to see if her most recent comment on a friend's blog had gotten any responses, when she saw it. There, under her comment, was a string of anonymous responses: "Jenny Franco is a fat cow!" "Moooo" "ROFLMAO" "Someone tell that girl to get her fat *** on a diet!" These could have been from anybody, even someone who acted nice to her in person! Jenny's friends told her not to let it bother her. "People will say anything online. Nobody pays attention to it," they reassured her. But now she lay on her bed, staring at the ceiling and wondering what other people said about her behind her back.

Life as a teenager can be painful. During hard times like what Tyra, Raymond, and Jenny are going through, teens often feel alone, misunderstood, and like nobody is listening. Whether you're the one with the problem or it's someone you know, no one should have to go through these times alone.

Anyone who is going through a tough time needs support from other people. Tyra doesn't need reprimands right now. What she needs is love and support. Raymond doesn't need to be told to man up and face his parents' divorce like it's no big deal. He needs to talk to people who are sympathetic and understand the pain he's experiencing. And Jenny doesn't need someone saying, "I told you so" about her weight. Right now, she needs to know that she's loved and accepted as-is. She needs an ally.

This chapter is about how people can use communication to help each other. The skills you'll be learning are designed to help you engage with others and work together to find real solutions to problems.

Cooperation is going to have a big role in this chapter. Along with courage, responsibility, respect and self-esteem, cooperation is one of the five essential qualities that will help you thrive in our democratic society.

> **co·op·er·a·tion** *noun* /koh-op-uh-'rey-shuhn/
> : Two or more people working together in a
> mutually supportive manner toward a common goal

One reason democratic societies often thrive while those based on dictatorship or lawlessness rarely ever survive is that **none of us is as smart as all of us**. When people work together cooperatively, problems are solved and civilizations are built. Likewise, a teen who learns to work cooperatively with others towards solving problems has a far greater chance of success than a teen who stands alone.

TEENS AND SELF-ESTEEM

es•teem *verb* /eh-'steem/

    1. : to have a high opinion of; to value

To have self-esteem: To have a high opinion of oneself

Self-esteem means having a high opinion of yourself, valuing yourself. You may have noticed that teens often don't think very highly of themselves; they have low self-esteem. They sometimes cover up feeling lousy about themselves by acting over-confident, like big shots or bullies. High self-esteem not only feels better, but it often helps teens meet challenges in a positive, productive way. It helps them overcome the obstacles that everyone runs into along the sometimes bumpy road of life. People with high self-esteem will usually find positive ways to solve problems and move forward.

where does self-esteem come from?

Self-esteem comes from a small town in Middle Earth where it's mined by robo cave dwellers. OK, not really. Self-esteem comes from a lot of different sources, some more lasting than others. But basically, there are three sources of self-esteem that work well for most people:

1. Belonging
We all have a basic need to belong, to be accepted, to be a significant part of a group.

2. Learning
As we learn, we enhance our power and our ability to influence the world around us.

3. Contributing
It feels good to give to others, contribute to a group, or use your learning and power for the common good.

Now, here's the cool part: These three basic goals work together like this:

The Golden Spiral of Success

THRIVING LEVEL

CONTRIBUTING

LEARNING

BELONGING

SURVIVING LEVEL

CONTRIBUTING

LEARNING

BELONGING

BIRTH HELPLESSNESS

When we feel like we belong, we have the right mind set for learning, and when we learn, we have something to contribute to others. And when we contribute to others, guess what? We feel more connected and our sense of belonging rises, continuing upward into a spiral that is sometimes called the *Golden Spiral of Success* because not only does your self-esteem go up, but as the cycle continues you actually become more successful in all areas of your life: with friends, family, school, work, community, you name it. When your self-esteem is based on belonging, learning, and contributing instead of money, awards, popularity, grades, and other external rewards, you have a solid foundation to meet the challenges of the world.

Of course, the Golden Spiral of Success doesn't just appear one day in the bottom of your cereal box. You have to build it one attitude and action at a time. How many of the following statements can you say truthfully about yourself?

BELONGING	LEARNING	CONTRIBUTING
"I am lovable."	**"I am capable."**	**"I have a lot to give."**
"I have friends."	"I learn from my mistakes."	"Others need me."
"I get along with others."	"I am improving."	"I like to pitch in."
"I am loved."	"I have dreams and talents."	"I like to give back."
"I matter."	"I can do good work."	"Your happiness matters to me."

FINDING THE EVIDENCE

Each of us is lovable, capable, and has a lot to offer. We can all belong, learn, and contribute. When we remember this and act on it, our self-esteem goes up and we're better able to handle life's challenges. When things don't go well, we sometimes forget this and our self-esteem drops. The following chart will help you remember your underlying value and build on it. Each week, fill in your responses to the questions.

BELONGING

	WHO LOVED OR LIKED ME THIS WEEK?	HOW DID THEY SHOW IT?
Week 1:		
Week 2:		
Week 3:		
Week 4:		

	WHO DID I LOVE OR LIKE THIS WEEK?	HOW DID I SHOW IT?
Week 1:		
Week 2:		
Week 3:		
Week 4:		

LEARNING

	WHAT'S ONE AREA IN WHICH I HAD A SUCCESS THIS WEEK?	HOW DID I DO IT?
Week 1:		
Week 2:		
Week 3:		
Week 4:		

Continued on next page

	WHAT'S ONE MISTAKE THAT I MADE THIS WEEK?	WHAT DID I LEARN FROM IT THAT WILL HELP ME BE MORE SUCCESSFUL IN THE FUTURE?
Week 1:		
Week 2:		
Week 3:		
Week 4:		

CONTRIBUTING

	WHO DID I HELP THIS WEEK?	WHAT DID I DO TO MAKE THEIR LIFE EASIER?
Week 1:		
Week 2:		
Week 3:		
Week 4:		

	WHAT GROUP DID I MAKE BETTER THIS WEEK?	WHAT DID I DO TO MAKE IT BETTER?
Week 1:		
Week 2:		
Week 3:		
Week 4:		

i am lovable, capable, and have a lot to give!

Read the following affirmation as though it's true for you right now. Then, if you would like it to be true, reread this every day and work on the actions that will make it true.

"I AM LOVABLE!"

I am lovable because I'm ME. I'm worthy of love and have the same right as everyone else to be accepted for myself. The challenge is to accept myself as I am. Self-acceptance is:

- recognizing that right now, just as I am, I'm already good enough.
- appreciating and building upon my positive personal strengths.
- learning to overcome personal weaknesses that are getting in my way, and
- accepting the weaknesses that I may not be able to overcome.

Remind yourself daily:
"I am lovable just as I am!"

"I AM CAPABLE!"

I'm capable. I believe in myself. I believe that I can handle myself and life's challenges. I have skills and gifts that I can develop with practice and work. I can learn. I will do my best until I eventually succeed.

Remind yourself daily:
"I am capable of doing many things, and I am capable of learning many more!"

"I HAVE A LOT TO GIVE!"

I have a lot to give. I have skills and talents that can benefit others and improve any group I'm a part of. I strive to treat others with compassion, fairness, and respect. I try to be encouraging, building others up rather than tearing them down.

lovable, capable, and giving words and statements

You can use the following words and statements with friends and family to help them feel that they are lovable, capable, and giving, too. Remember, people who feel lovable, capable, and giving when they're with you are more likely to seek you out as a friend and someone they want to spend time with. Add your own ideas to the ones listed here.

Words and actions that say, *"I like who you are."*

WORDS	ACTIONS
"You are important! "	Listen, give attention
"I love you."	Hug, hold, kiss (if appropriate)
"I'm glad you're here."	Shake hands, smile, pat on back, sit beside
"You're awesome."	Share something you value, sit beside, invite over
"I'm glad you're my friend."	Spend time with, send a letter or e-mail
"Thanks for being you."	Tell the person something special about him/her
"Thanks for helping."	Tell the person how s/he contributed
_____	_____
_____	_____
_____	_____
_____	_____

Ways of telling someone, *"I like the things you do."*

TO PEERS	TO PARENTS
"Nice work."	"Thanks."
"Way to go."	"I like the way you did that."
"That is very cool."	"I appreciate that you did that for me."
"Thanks for helping me!"	"Thanks for helping me!"
"Wow! You did it!"	"Dinner was great tonight."
"You're the best!"	"You're the best!"
_____	_____
_____	_____
_____	_____
_____	_____

COMMUNICATION: THE ROAD TO COOPERATION

Solving problems cooperatively, building cooperative relationships, and getting along well with others all require effective communication. When we communicate effectively, focus on the problem to be solved, and encourage ourselves and others, we can work together effectively on anything with anyone, from a sports team to a best friend. And since communication is a skill, we can improve it with knowledge and practice.

the gift of problems

Most people regard problems as a bad thing. But there's a positive side to problems. They provide the motivation for most of our advances in life. Faced with problems, we develop cures for diseases, invent alternative fuel sources, improve transportation, and so much more. In fact, you could say that humans are the problem-solving species. It's what we do best, and when we do it, we grow.

Fortunately for us, there is no shortage of problems. They will happen despite our best efforts. A terrific kid will make a terrible choice or circumstances beyond anyone's control will bring bad things to good people. One way or another, we will all be gifted with the opportunity of problems.

The difference between successful families and those that seem to endlessly struggle is not the presence or absence of problems; it's that some families are better at solving their problems, learning from experience, and moving on. The same is true for teenagers. Problems are a

natural and expected part of growing up, and so is learning from problems and developing the skills to solve them.

That doesn't mean we shouldn't work to prevent problems. Problem prevention provides a learning experience, too, and one that is often less costly than allowing the problem to occur.

Much of this book is organized around the concept of handling problems. We'll begin by looking at ways to build cooperative relationships with parents, peers, and others. Communication skills will be presented as we continue to stress the need for participation and mutual respect in handling problems successfully.

mixed messages

Communication involves much more than just what you say. In fact, everything you communicate is conveyed to your audience on three separate channels:

The Three Channels of Communication

1. Your words

2. Your tone of voice, and

3. Your body language (hand gestures, posture, facial expressions, etc.)

When you communicate factual information, such as a homework assignment, your words carry most of the message. However, when you're communicating about a problem or another emotionally charged issue, more of the message is carried by body language, followed by tone of voice and lastly, the words themselves. So how you say something is often more important than what you say.

When all three channels of communication carry the same message, communication is very clear and powerful. However, when you say one thing with your words and something else with your tone and/or body language, you send a mixed message. Mixed messages not only dilute the strength of the message; they often confuse the listener.

For example, your mom asks you to clean up your mess in the den and you mumble, "OK, I'll do it later" while lying on the couch and never looking up from the magazine you're reading. What are you really communicating? "I'll do it if I think about it, but it really isn't a big deal to me, so I'll probably forget about it, and you'll get angry like you usually do." Now, which communication do you think your mom receives more clearly: your words or your tone of voice and body language? Bingo! This may be why she responds with annoyance or even anger.

On the other hand, what if you were to put down your magazine, look your mother in the eye, and say sincerely, "Oh, OK, I'll take care of it in five minutes." Your message would be carried on all three channels very clearly. Your communication would be clear and powerful. Your mom might faint from shock, but there is no way she could get angry.

let's be clear on this

To produce clear and powerful communication, the words you say must match your facial expression, the tone of your voice, and your body language. Next time you talk to someone, check:

1. Where are your eyes looking?

2. What direction is your body facing?

3. What is your tone of voice?

4. Does your tone match your message?

Notice what happens during this communication. Are you happy with the result? If not, you may want to practice using a different tone of voice or body language until you get all three channels to send the same message.

AVOIDING COMMUNICATION BLOCKS

Most people are pretty sensitive about how they come across to others. They don't want to look foolish or feel insignificant. If you're trying to win someone's cooperation, it's important that you communicate in ways that keep the lines of communication open. This means you need to guard against saying or doing anything that might block communication and prompt the other person to withdraw.

A communication block is any combination of words, tone of voice or body language that influences a person sharing a problem to end the communication.

Because you communicate your attitude largely through tone of voice and body language, it's not enough just to watch your words. You have to actually adopt a supportive, non-judgmental attitude if you're really going to help. Look at the list of common communication blocks on pages 58-59. Each communication block in the left column represents a way that we may disregard another person's thoughts and feelings and instead focus on controlling the situation. More often than not, these attempts backfire.

When a friend is in pain, she needs to know that someone else cares and feels the pain with her. Rather than trying to take over and provide a solution or to take away your friend's pain, instead make it your goal to offer a caring ear, support, and encouragement and to help your friend find a useful solution for herself. For example:

A basketball teammate is having a bad streak and has cost the team a lot of points in recent games. The coach and most of his teammates are on his back. He seems very discouraged as he slumps next to you on the courtside bench. What should you do?

a. Deliver a little "pep talk" about how he's letting down the team and he really ought to try harder.

b. Say, "Nice going, dude" with a sarcastic tone.

c. Offer some encouragement and help him think through ways he can improve on his own.

Best answer: C. Your teammate needs to know that you're on his side and that you have his back when times are bad. He's getting enough flack from others. He doesn't need more from you. He might also appreciate some fresh ideas to get him thinking about what he can do differently. Try another one:

Your dad notices that you're feeling bad about something but doesn't know what. He asks, "What's wrong, kiddo?" What should you do?

a. Mutter, "Nothing," and go to your room to hide out.

b. Say, "Who, me? Not a thing. I'm fine." and force yourself to smile.

c. Actually tell him a little about what's bothering you.

Best answer: C. OK, we're making this pretty easy, but the point is that with answers A or B, you would block communication when it would have been more useful to give your dad a chance to help. You don't have to share everything that's going on. Just open the door of communication a little, and you may find the support you need.

The first step is to notice which communication blocks you use most often. We all have them, and once we recognize that, we can be on guard. When you find yourself using a communication block, catch yourself with a smile, apologize, and make a change.

COMMUNICATION BLOCKS

BLOCK	EXAMPLE	WHY TEENS USE IT	HOW THE OTHER PERSON HEARS IT
Commanding	"What you should do is..." "Stop complaining!"	To control the situation; To provide quick solutions	"You don't have the right to decide how to handle your own problems."
Giving advice	"I've got a really good idea..." "Why don't you..."	To solve the problem for the other person	"You don't have the good sense to come up with your own solutions."
Placating	"It isn't as bad as it seems." "Everything will be OK."	To take away the other's pain; To make him feel better	"You don't have a right to your feelings. You can't handle discomfort."
Interrogating	"What did you do to make him…"	To get to the bottom of the problem and find out what the person did wrong	"It's your fault. You must have messed up somewhere."
Distracting	"Let's not worry about that."	To protect the person from the problem by changing the subject	"I don't think you can stand the discomfort long enough to find a real solution."
Psychologizing	"Do you know why you said that?" "You're just being oversensitive."	To help prevent future problems by analyzing the behavior and explaining his motives	"I know more about you than you know about yourself. Therefore, I'm superior to you."
Judging	"Why were you doing that in the first place?" "That wasn't a very smart thing to do."	To help the person realize what she did wrong	"You have poor judgment. You don't make good decisions."
Being sarcastic	"Well, I guess that's just about the end of the world."	To show the person how wrong her attitudes or behaviors are by making her feel ridiculous	"You are ridiculous."
Moralizing	"The right thing to do would be..." "You really should..."	To show the person the proper way to deal with the problem	"I'll choose your values for you."
Being a know-it-all	"Everybody knows that when something like this happens, you…"	To show the person how smart you are	"I'm smarter and more competent than you are."
Focusing on mistakes	"I don't think you should have said that."	To help the other person learn what she did wrong	"There is more wrong with you than right."
Negative expectations	"Now, don't blow it this time." "I know you won't remember to…"	To get them to do the right thing with guilt or "reverse psychology"	"I have very little confidence in you." "Surely you couldn't get any worse."
"Yes, but…"	"Yes, but I tried to tell him!"	Protect self-esteem	"I've already tried everything, so don't think you can help me."

Continued on next page

COMMUNICATION BLOCKS (CONTINUED)

BLOCK	EXAMPLE	WHY TEENS USE IT	HOW THE OTHER PERSON HEARS IT
Asking for advice	"What do you think I should do?"	To get someone else to	"I don't trust my own thinking and if I can get you to tell me what to do, at least I can blame someone else if it doesn't work out so I won't have to take responsibility myself."
Brush off	"I'm OK. Don't worry about it."	To show he can handle problems on his own	"I don't trust you to be of any real help."
Non-verbal blocks	Eye roll	Self-protection	"I don't think you are worth listening to."
	Distraction	To avoid a touchy subject	"I don't think you are worth listening to."
	Apathy	Pretending not to care	"I don't care about your problem."

MY "FAVORITE" COMMUNICATION BLOCKS

BLOCK	EXAMPLE	WHY I USE IT	HOW THE OTHER PERSON HEARS IT

ACTIVE COMMUNICATION

So we've learned that whether you're helping someone, accepting help, or working on your own problem, the first step is to avoid communication blocks (Yes, you can block your own communication process by thinking negatively about yourself!). The next step is to become a positive influence through communication. A five-step process called *Active Communication* can help you do this. Use it to win cooperation while helping yourself or others solve problems more effectively.

> **The Five Steps of Active Communication**
>
> 1. Listen actively.
>
> 2. Listen for feelings.
>
> 3. Look for alternatives and evaluate consequences.
>
> 4. Offer encouragement.
>
> 5. Follow up later.

1. Listen actively.

Listening is the most important communication skill of all. It also may be the most challenging to learn. Active listening takes a great deal of practice and effort and requires both attention and thought.

Have you ever thought you were listening to someone but when the person suddenly asked you a question, you realized you really hadn't been listening at all? You may have been looking at the person, but you were really thinking about something else. Most people don't take this well, especially if they're telling you about a problem or something else they consider important.

Just becoming aware that you're not listening actively is a move in the right direction. Then you can take steps to improve your listening skills. It helps to use body language. Next time someone is talking to you, try this:

- **Make good eye contact.** You don't want to stare the other person down, but you need to look him or her in the eye at least part of the time.

- **Make occasional comments** about what's being said: "Wow!" "Really?" "That must have hurt!" Be sure the comments match the speaker's tone. It's usually not a good idea to make a joke if the person is telling you about something that's very important to him or her. A sense of humor can come in handy, but only if you use it at the right times.

- **Nod your head occasionally** to let the person know you're hearing what he or she is saying. Let your facial expression mirror the speaker's facial expression as you really try to feel what she is feeling.

- **Give the speaker your FULL ATTENTION.** Don't tap your fingers or keep turning your head to watch television in the middle of a conversation. Don't suddenly change the subject.

- **Keep your own talk to a minimum.** When your mouth is open, your ears don't work as well. So listen more and talk less.

Always keep in mind that the most sought-out conversationalists are those who listen actively and are more interested in what the other person has to say than what they themselves have to say.

2. Listen for feelings.

Feelings have been around for as long as there have been humans. The ability to recognize feelings in ourselves and in others has been shown to be a key part of success. It's also part of is the concept known as *emotional intelligence*. People who are better able to understand others' emotions can build stronger relationships and cooperate more easily with other people.

You can help strengthen your emotional intelligence by listening to your own feelings and to the feelings of others. To do this, you have to "read between the lines" of what people say, because they probably won't come right out and tell you what they're feeling. Listen closely to their tone of voice and watch their face, hands, and posture. By listening in this way, you'll not only pick up a lot of information about the other person; you'll also communicate a very powerful message: You care.

When you have an idea of what the other person is feeling, reflect those feelings back to him. You become what psychologists call an *emotional mirror*. Mirrors don't judge how we look or tell us what to do. They just reflect what is there. When you act as a mirror, you reflect the other person's feelings and connect them to what he or she is saying:

"This is pretty scary for you, isn't it, Tyra?"

"Raymond, you sound angry at me for being late."

"You're worried about what the other kids really think about your weight, aren't you, Jenny?"

It's important that you not only identify what the person is feeling, but also actually allow yourself to feel some of the feeling yourself. This ability to put oneself in another's shoes is called *empathy*. When you identify with another person's feelings, something interesting happens: the other person's head nods "yes," her eyes show recognition, and she continues talking. Your job is to keep listening, empathizing, and reflecting back her feelings.

How can you tell what another person is feeling? Watch and listen for clues.

1. The speaker says "I" or "me" combined with feeling words.

"I'm really mad at her."

"That upset me a lot."

"I'm so excited I can hardly wait!"

2. **The speaker's actions in her story illustrate what she was feeling.**

    "I cried when she told me."

    "I slammed my door and turned my music up as loud as it would go."

    "When I saw him coming, I decided to get out of there as fast as I could."

3. **The speaker's body language shows how she's feeling: crying, laughing, scowling, standing stiffly with arms crossed.**

    "My dog got killed by a car yesterday."

    "I studied really hard and got an 'A.'"

    "Guess what? We're going to Disney World!"

4. **If the speaker tells you something and you don't understand how he or she feels about it, try asking. You could also make a comment about what you think she's feeling.**

Speaker says:	*"My aunt is coming to stay with us for a while."*
You ask:	*"Are you looking forward to it?"*
Speaker says:	*"I got a job raking leaves."*
You comment:	*"I bet you'll be glad to have some extra money."*
Speaker says:	*"My family is going to move in the spring"*
You ask:	*"Are you worried?"*

Empathy can take other forms:

"I don't know what I'd do if something bad happened to my dog."

"I would have been really proud if I'd gotten an 'A'."

"I can tell you're really excited about your trip!"

Sometimes empathy doesn't require any words at all. You can use body language, instead:

- Mirror the other person's feelings with your facial expression.

- Give the other person a hug or put your arm around his or her shoulders.

- Use a facial expression that says, "I understand. I know what it's like. I'm sorry you're going through this."

feeling words

As you practice looking for the right words to describe your own feelings or mirror those of someone you want to help, you'll find that your "feeling word" vocabulary increases and the job gets easier. This list will help you with the process.

TO EXPRESS PLEASANT FEELINGS		TO EXPRESS UNPLEASANT FEELINGS	
accepted	hopeful	afraid	jealous
adventurous	important	angry	let down
calm	joyful	anxious	lonely
caring	loving	ashamed	overwhelmed
cheerful	peaceful	defeated	rejected
comfortable	playful	disappointed	remorseful
confident	proud	embarrassed	resentful
eager	relieved	frustrated	suspicious
encouraged	secure	guilty	uncomfortable
free	successful	hopeless	unloved
glad	understood	hurt	unsure
happy	loved	impatient	worried
King of the world		Down in the dumps	
Like a million bucks		Got the blues	
Walking on air		Freaked out	
A-OK		Burned out	
Right as rain		Out of sorts	

VIDEO PRACTICE: RESPONDING TO FEELINGS

If you are participating in a *Teens in Action* or *Families in Action* program, you may be completing the following video practice exercise in your group. If you're reading this guide on your own, you can skip this page.

SCENE	TEEN'S FEELING	YOUR RESPONSE
1. Alex		
2. Jada		
3. Derrick		
4. Justin		
5. Julie		
6. Matt		
7. Miranda		

This exercise accompanies the video "Video Practice: Responding to Feelings" in Session 4 of the T*eens in Action* video, a component of the *Active Parenting of Teens: Families in Action* video and discussion program. Check out our web site for information: **www.ActiveParenting.com/FIA**

3. Look for alternatives and evaluate consequences.

Until the executive part of the brain is fully developed, teens are likely to choose the first solution to a problem that occurs to them, without pausing to consider the pros and cons of their other options. Sometimes the first solution is not the best. So the next step of Active Communication is to look at a number of possible solutions to the problem and consider how well each of them might work.

When you're helping someone solve a problem, this step might begin with you asking simple questions such as:

"What can you do about that?"

"What else could you try?"

Then you can lead the person to predict the consequences of each alternative by asking:

"What do you think would happen if you did that?"

It's best for the person with the problem to come up with the alternatives on his or her own. This will help the person develop problem-solving skills and a sense of responsibility for the problem. However, if the person you're helping can't think of any possible solutions, you can gently suggest some to keep the process moving. Be very careful in these cases not to take over or suggest that your way is the best way.

4. Offer encouragement.

Encouragement is one of the most powerful methods of motivating ourselves or others. Some of the most effective ways people can encourage themselves or others are:

Focus on strengths: *"I really like that idea!"*

Show confidence: *"I think you're going to work this out."*

Spur independence: *"I know you can do it."*

Value the person as-is: *"Just remember, no matter how it works out, you're still a great guy."*

Using one or more of these methods as step four of Active Communication, you can inject a little encouragement into the problem-solving process. It can give a little boost in courage when it's most needed.

Read more about encouragement and how to use the four methods in Chapter 4.

This last step of Active Communication takes place after the problem has been addressed. You and the person you were helping can gain a tremendous amount of insight by talking about how the problem turned out. First, ask how he or she handled the problem and what happened as a result:

"How did it go with…?"

"Remember that talk we had about _____ the other day? I was wondering how it turned out."

This follow-up helps you both learn from the experience and validates that your interest was genuine. If the results were good, then a little encouragement from you is all that is required:

"That's great! I knew you could do it."

However, if the results weren't that great and the problem still exists, or if new ones were created, then you can begin the Active Communication process over again by addressing your friend's feelings and helping him or her find another solution.

ACTIVE COMMUNICATION IN ZOMBIEWORLD

WRITTEN BY MICHAEL H. POPKIN. ART BY JOSEBA MORALES.

IN A WORLD WHERE CHAOS REIGNS... WHERE NIGHTMARES HAVE COME TO LIFE... WHERE THINGS ARE JUST WAY MESSED UP... THRONGS OF FLESH-EATING ZOMBIES SHAMBLE THROUGH THE STREETS, MINDLESSLY FEEDING ON ANYTHING THAT LIVES. EARTH IS THE PROVINCE OF THE UNDEAD! THE FUTURE OF OUR CIVILIZATION IS IN THE HANDS OF THE MEAGER FEW LIVING, BREATHING HUMANS WHO REMAIN. BUT HOW WILL THEY SURVIVE IN ZOMBIEWORLD?

HEY, YOU'RE NOT A ZOMBIE!

WHAT WAS YOUR FIRST CLUE?

WELL, YOUR SKIN ISN'T GRAY. ALL YOUR LIMBS ARE SECURELY ATTACHED TO YOUR BODY. YOU AREN'T TRYING TO EAT ME, AND--

OK, OK, FORGET I ASKED.

I'LL GO A STEP FURTHER AND POSTULATE THAT YOU'RE FEELING A LITTLE SUSPICIOUS OF STRANGERS.

BINGO. ON THAT NOTE, IT'S BEEN GREAT KNOWING YOU. SEE YA 'ROUND.

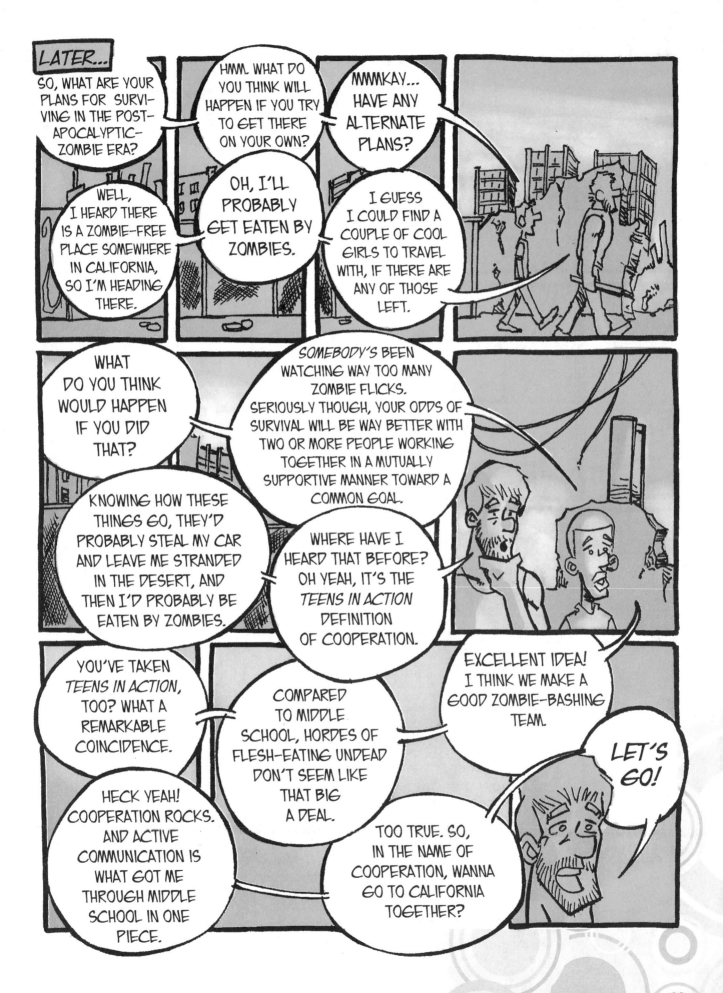

THE END

ACTIVE COMMUNICATION ROLE PLAYS

The following examples are good for practicing the five steps of Active Communication with other teens in a *Teens in Action* group or with parents in a *Families in Action* group. If you're not in a group, read the examples as if you were helping a friend and think about how you would use the five steps.

ROLE PLAY #1

Will, age twelve, is discouraged when other boys pick on him because he's small for his age. Today at school a boy called him "Frodo" and trailed after him quoting lines from *The Lord of the Rings*. When Will yelled at him to leave him alone, the older boy challenged him to a fight. Will turned and walked away, and the boy called after him, shouting slurs and squawking like a chicken. That afternoon, when Will comes home from school, his mother asks, "How was your day?" Will mutters, "I'm never going to school again," and heads straight to his room, shutting the door behind him.

ROLE PLAY #2

Dana, age thirteen, lives in a neighborhood in which some of the kids her age and older are in gangs. Her parents have talked to her about not getting mixed up with that, but that was getting harder. Today at school, a girl named Christy demanded that Dana give her five dollars. Everyone knows Christy is with a gang now. When Dana told her she didn't have any money, Christy threatened to beat her up. Finally she left, saying, "You better have something to give me tomorrow. I've got a lot of friends you don't want to meet." Dana felt humiliated but mostly scared for the rest of the school day. On the bus ride home, she imagines a life in which Christy demands more and more from her every day. With her gang buddies backing her up, Christy could get away with anything. By the time Dana gets home, she's wondering if maybe she needs to join a gang herself if only to be safe from girls like Christy. One of Dana's parents notices her grim expression and begins a conversation with her about it.

ROLE PLAY #3

David, age fourteen, was planning to get together with some friends tonight to play video games, but instead they've invited him to a party in the woods where there's supposed to be beer and pot. When he tells them he'd better not because he's trying to stick to his family's

Continued on next page

"No Use" agreement, they tease him and tell him he's going to miss the party of the century because his mommy won't let him go. When he says it's not like that, they laugh and one of them says, "Just come and let your parents think we're playing video games." David really doesn't know what he's going to do. When he gets home from school he's acting grumpy. His parent notices and says, "You're sure in a lousy mood today. I thought you'd be all excited because it's Friday and you're planning to go out with the guys tonight." In response, David mumbles, "That's the problem…"

ROLE PLAY #4

Jasmine, age fifteen, went to a sleepover party at a girlfriend's house. After the parents went to sleep, one of the girls lit a joint and passed it around. All of the other girls smoked it. When it got to Jasmine, she didn't know what to do. She thought smoking pot was a bad idea, but she also didn't want to be the only one at the party who didn't do it. She imagined how disappointed her friends would be if she said "no thanks." It would probably change things between them forever. Jasmine took the joint and smoked. But she felt troubled about it for the rest of the sleepover, wondering what would happen if her parents or anyone else found out what she had done. Her parents had made a big point of explaining why she should never smoke pot, and Jasmine had thought she understood and agreed with them. She felt very confused. The next day, when her father (or mother) picks her up at her friend's house, she is quiet and tense as she gets into the car.

ROLE PLAY #5

On Saturday night, sixteen-year-old Lauren went to a school dance with Jacob. Lauren was excited about the date because Jacob is good-looking and popular, and a lot of girls have their eye on him. Lauren had a great time at the dance, but on the way home, Jacob stopped the car on a dark street and pressured Lauren into making out with him. Lauren hadn't wanted to do that on a first date, but she went along with it because she was afraid that Jacob would tell the whole school she was a prude. He became more and more demanding, and finally Lauren grew so uncomfortable that she pushed him away and demanded that he take her home. Jacob told her that if he took her home now, he'd never ask her out again. He drove her home in silence, let her out of the car and raced away. When her parents called "How'd it go?" from the den, Lauren just yelled, "Fine," and went to her room to be alone. The next morning, Lauren's mother can tell right away that Lauren has been crying and that she's very upset about something.

FAMILY ENRICHMENT ACTIVITY: GETTING TO KNOW YOUR PARENTS BETTER

Sometimes parents and teens stop seeing each other as individuals. Teens may view parents as authority figures or meal-preparers. Parents may view teens as mess-makers or money-burners. This week we're asking you to interview one another to learn more about the other person as an individual.

Use the questions on the next two pages to guide your interview. The first set of questions (on page 74) is for you to answer before interviewing your parent. Write your responses based on what you think you know about your parent. The second set (page 75) is for you to use during the interview. Write your parent's response to each question. After the interview, compare your answers to your parent's answers. How well did you do?

Try to have some fun. Let the questions lead to storytelling, jokes, or random discussion. That's all part of getting to know your parent better.

PARENT INTERVIEW
QUESTIONS FOR TEENS TO <u>ANSWER</u>

Decide who you're going to interview: one or both of your parents. Then, BEFORE you conduct the interview, write your answers to these questions.

1. Who is your parent's best friend?

2. What does your parent like about her or his best friend?

3. What does your parent like most about teenagers?

4. What accomplishment does your parent feel most proud of?

5. What does your parent worry about most concerning you and your brothers and sisters?

6. What do you do that drives your parent crazy?

7. What does your parent hope you will accomplish in your lifetime?

PARENT INTERVIEW
QUESTIONS FOR TEENS TO <u>ASK</u>

Interview one or both of your parents, using the following questions.
Write down their answers as you go.

1. Who is your best friend?

2. What do you like about your best friend?

3. What do you like most about teenagers?

4. What accomplishment do you feel most proud of?

5. What do you worry about most concerning me (and my brothers and sisters)?

6. What do I do that drives you crazy?

7 What do you hope I will accomplish in my lifetime?

HOME ACTIVITIES

An important part of what you get out of this program is what you do at home between sessions. So don't forget to do your Home Activities!

1. Read Chapter 3 of this guide.

2. Complete the "Finding the Evidence" chart on pages 49-50. Think about your positive qualities, and remember to give yourself the self-affirming message on page 51.

3. Complete the "Lovable, Capable, and Helpful Words and Statements" exercise on page 52.

4. Finish filling in the "My Favorite Communication Blocks" chart on page 58.

5. Make an effort to recognize at least one way you might be discouraging others or yourself, and replace the discouraging behavior with encouraging behavior.

6. Interview one or both of your parents, using the questions on pages 74–75. If you have time, you can ask your parents to interview you, as well.

7. Answer the "Teen Action Report" questions for Chapter 2 on pages 76–77.

TEEN ACTION REPORT

Write your responses to the following questions on a separate sheet of paper or in a journal.

about yourself

1. When during the past week have you felt lovable, capable, and giving?

2. Are you listening for feelings when you communicate? What examples of connecting feelings to content have you come across this week?

3. Which of the three channels of communication (words, tone, gestures) do you feel is your strongest? Which do you think you need to work on the most?

about your family

1. What communication blocks do you notice yourself using in your family? How have you avoided using them sometimes?

2. Do you use words and statements to help family members and friends feel lovable, capable, and giving? If so, what do you say to them? Use the area below to write down some ideas for how you can do this.

WHAT I CAN DO TO HELP

Person	Words, statements, or actions you will use to make this person feel lovable and capable
_____	_____
_____	_____
_____	_____
_____	_____

about your school

1. Do you feel lovable, capable, and giving at school? What happens at school to make you feel that way (or not feel that way)? How do you contribute to the feeling?

2. How do people at school use the three channels of communication: words, body language, and tone of voice? What examples of "mixed" messages have you noticed?

3. What are some of your positive personal qualities that you can remind yourself about when your self-esteem is drooping?

CHAPTER 3
RESPONSIBILITY AND DISCIPLINE

Karen, 15

Karen, fifteen, likes a boy at school. Her friends are convinced he's bad news. They don't like the way he puts her down, and he's started talking her into skipping school. Karen protests that they don't know him well enough, that really he's very sweet.

Darnell, 13

Darnell, thirteen, has no interest in doing the few jobs his mom has given him to help out around the apartment. She fusses at him about it but usually gives up after a while and does the chores herself. She figures it's easier than reminding him a dozen times. Still, cleaning up after a teenage boy is getting pretty annoying, especially since she works full time.

Lisa, 14

Lately Lisa, fourteen, has become a lot more interested in socializing than in schoolwork , and her grades show it. Her parents are constantly on her case, but it does little good. She will study for a few minutes then get online to see what her friends are up to. When Lisa's parents ask her about her grades, Lisa complains she's bored at school. "The teachers are boring. The classes are boring. School is just a great big bore."

WHAT IS RESPONSIBILITY?

Most people would agree that the teens in the above situations aren't behaving responsibly. But what does "responsibility" really mean, and why is it worth having, anyway?

Responsibility means:

- Accepting your obligations
- Doing the right thing as the situation calls for it
- Accepting accountability for your actions

1. Accepting Your Obligations

There are times in all of our lives when we'd rather not do something we feel obligated to do. Parents often sacrifice their own immediate desires for the long-term benefit of their families. The same is true for being a good friend, family member, student, or member of any group. It's a trade: the group gives you something positive like friendship, safety, or stability, and in exchange you give it your loyalty. That's obligation. When Devon doesn't do his chores, he's failing to meet his obligation to his mother (to help out around the house). When a teenager complains "Why do I have to go?" when told she must attend a family wedding, she's putting her own desires ahead of the group's. Fulfilling our obligations is part of what keeps relationships, families, and even communities and countries, strong. Sometimes obligations aren't fun. It takes courage to pass up some of the fun stuff in life, but it will pay off in the long run. By fulfilling your obligations to friends and family, you become the kind of person others can count on.

2. Doing the Right Thing as the Situation Calls for It

Learning the difference between right and wrong is a key part of growing up. As teens earn the freedom to make decisions by themselves, they also take on the responsibility to determine what's right in any given situation. This is not always easy. For example, most people would readily agree that it's right to obey the law. Yet when Dr. Martin Luther King, Jr., broke the segregation laws of Alabama during the Civil Rights Movement, we recognized his actions as not only responsible but also moral and courageous. Over time, people came to discover that the laws were wrong, and Dr. King was right.

Taking time to talk with other teens and adults about right and wrong in real-life situations is the best way to grapple with these difficult issues. Challenging your own beliefs as you expand your conceptions about right and wrong is also an act of responsibility and courage. Of course, once you recognize the right thing to do in a given situation, the real measure of responsibility is in your willingness to follow through.

3. Accepting Accountability for Your Actions

At the very core of responsibility is the idea that what happens to you results from decisions you make. Sometimes this is a difficult thing to accept. It's much easier to blame our problems on other people or circumstances, or to make excuses. But this prevents us from learning to make better decisions in the future. After all, if it wasn't my fault, why should I think about what I could do differently next time?

For example, when Lisa's grades drop because she's socializing too much and studying too little, she blames it on her "boring" teachers. This isn't likely to help Lisa improve her grades, since she can't control her teachers' personalities. But what if she took responsibility and said to herself, "You know, there's a lot of boring stuff in those classes, but I want to do well in school, so I'd better study harder anyway. Maybe I can even make some study dates so it'll be more fun." When teens accept responsibility for what happens to them, they learn to prevent or solve their own problems.

You can think of responsibility as a formula:

$$R = C + C$$

Responsibility = Choice + Consequences

This formula covers all three aspects of responsibility, since "Choice" includes the choice to meet or not meet one's obligations and the choice of right or wrong.

why responsibility is worth the effort

Okay, so behaving responsibly takes a lot of effort and some self-sacrifice. Is it worth it? YES! And for three good reasons:

3 GOOD REASONS WHY RESPONSIBILITY IS WORTH THE EFFORT

1. **Group success:** When members of a group behave responsibly, the entire group runs better and is more likely to succeed.

2. **Personal improvement:** When you accept responsibility for your choices, you learn from your mistakes and improve.

3. **More freedom:** When you behave responsibly, it demonstrates that you can handle the freedom you've been given and are ready for more. In other words, you earn more freedom.

freedom and responsibility: two sides of the same coin

FRONT  BACK

If you want a better feeling for how that last point works—how you could earn freedom by behaving responsibly—imagine* a coin with the word "Freedom" on one side and "Responsibility" on the other. These two concepts are truly "two sides of the same coin." Teens who make good choices and behave responsibly tend to end up with more freedom and privileges than those who don't.

* Or you can get a real one from your group leader if you're participating in a *Teens in Action* or *Families in Action* program.

how to build responsibility

We've established that behaving responsibly will pay off. Now it's up to you to make it happen. Building responsibility is not something you can do all at once. You have to be on the lookout for opportunities. A few guidelines:

Make friends with your mistakes. Don't be afraid to admit you're wrong. Instead, own up to your mistakes, apologize if necessary and, when possible, make amends. Then think about how you will handle the situation differently next time it comes up, and make it a point to do so! Along the same lines…

Don't kick yourself when you're down. If you punish yourself for mistakes, you're likely to end up blaming others or making excuses for your future mistakes. Instead, try to…

Practice *active remorse*. That means you feel bad for what you've done, but rather than lingering regretfully on your mistakes, you accept the consequences, learn what they have to teach, and resolve not to repeat the mistake.

Don't fall victim to the idea that you should only do what you like doing. Sometimes to have joy in your life you have to do some things that you don't really like. By sacrificing some of your enjoyment in the present, you increase the likelihood that you'll enjoy a lot more in the future.

Parents and other adults will also have a role in building your responsibility. They can help keep you on track by reminding you that responsibility is your key to earning more freedom. And they can provide respectful discipline to help you learn from your mistakes and improve from experience.

the power of apology

Everybody messes up occasionally. Sometimes we end up annoying or even hurting others. When one of these people offers to help us correct the behavior so we can learn and grow from the experience (otherwise known as *discipline)*, we may choose to react in a number of ways:

a. **Get defensive and resist.** *"Me?! What about you?!"*

b. **Blame or make excuses.** *"It's not my fault."*

c. **Apologize, offer to make amends, and make an effort to change.**
"You're right. That was disrespectful. I'm sorry. How can I make it up to you?"

Choices *A* and *B* are pretty common, but they don't work very well. In fact, they usually lead to *more* conflict and bad feelings. Answer *C* takes more courage. When you sincerely give an apology—especially when it's backed up with action—it reduces anger on both sides and frees you up to learn from your mistakes.

THE EXCUSES GAME

If you're participating in a *Teens in Action* or *Families in Action* program, you'll be doing this activity with your group, but you can also complete it on your own.

Often we seek to avoid responsibility by blaming others or making excuses. It's good to be on guard against these two enemies of responsibility. This game is designed to make you more aware of the tendency to use excuses. It also helps to illustrate how silly and implausible excuses can sound!

What are *your* favorite excuses?

People come up with some pretty funny excuses for why they do or don't do things. See how creative you can be as you come up with an excuse in response to each of the following questions.

1. **Why isn't your room clean? I sent you in to clean it two hours ago!**

   My excuse: _____

2. **Where is your homework?**

   My excuse: _____

3. **Why are you late for dinner?**

   My excuse: _____

4. **What happened to your math book?**

   My excuse: _____

5. **Why didn't you answer your cell phone when I called?**

   My excuse: _____

6. **Why aren't the dishes done yet? It's almost 9 o'clock!**

   My excuse: _____

7. **Why didn't you tell me your friend's parents weren't going to be home when you were sleeping over?**

   My excuse: _____

Now, let's meet your opponent, Ms. Responsibility. Are you ready to refute Ted's excuses, Ms. R?

I sure am!
I don't buy it, Ted. You knew the full moon was coming, yet you failed to take any action that would have resulted in a different outcome from the last four times you went on a rampage. Bottom line: you aren't learning from your mistakes. At this rate, you're going to wind up in serious trouble.

Ding, ding ding, ding!

Ouch! Good job, Ms. R. You busted all four of Ted's excuses. Plus you get a bonus for pointing out the consequences of Ted's actions if he continues.

Can you come back from that, Ted? Do you have any more excuses to make?

Gosh, I don't know if I want to go there...

You can do it, Ted!

GO THERE! GO THERE!

Ok, ok... First, it's not my fault I'm a werewolf.

I didn't ask for this condition. I can't help myself.

Like the old song says, "Moonlight becomes me."

Another blazing trail of excuses for Ted!

Written by Michael H. Popkin. Art by Juan Chavarriga.

DISCIPLINE: LEARN TO LOVE IT

Discipline has gotten a bad rap. The word itself comes from the Latin *disciplina*, which means "teacher," "learning," and "knowledge"—all good things, right? Unfortunately, discipline has become associated with its medieval definition, which includes "punishment," "suffering," and even "martyrdom"—not such good things. The *Families in Action* program teaches parents to think "Latin" when using discipline to help *teach* their children instead of punish them. We hope that your parents are using these skills with you, but even if they're not, you can use them to help teach yourself (*self-discipline*) and others (*assertiveness*). These discipline methods are respectful, not meant to hurt anyone, and really work a lot better than those more in-your-face types of discipline that were popular during the middle ages.

What do they work better at teaching? In a word, responsibility. Why do we need help in learning responsibility? This would be a good time for you to read the graphic story "Lessons from the *Titanic*" on page 95. Go read it now. We'll wait.

The point of that story is that we all sometimes need a little help to "cut our engines" and make good choices. Parents and other adults can help us learn these lessons while we're young, so we'll make fewer mistakes when we're older. This is especially important during the teen years, when our desire for adventure often exceeds our ability to make good decisions. (Remember the lesson in brain development from Chapter 1?)

If you're fortunate enough to have caring adults in your life who take the time to provide discipline and help you learn responsibility, you're ahead of the game. You may not always like them restricting your freedom, but remember the coin with "Freedom" on one side and "Responsibility" on the other. With freedom comes responsibility, and vice versa. If you allow yourself to learn what your parents are trying to teach, you'll come out ahead in the long run.

It's a good idea for you to learn how to use discipline in a teaching way. But first you have to stop thinking of discipline as something only authority figures do. The reality is that respectful methods of discipline are used by many types of people in many different situations. *You* can use them, too. The methods of discipline we'll be presenting here can help you solve problems by influencing others to change their behavior. For that matter, you can use the methods to influence *yourself* to change your *own* behavior.

We'll start with **basic discipline methods**: a trio of communication techniques that increase in assertiveness from mild to firm. When you want to change a behavior—your own or someone else's—start with the first, and if it doesn't work, move on to the second and then the third. They are:

Polite requests
"I" messages
Firm reminders

polite requests

Not every problem requires firm discipline or a lot of discussion. Just asking politely may be enough to influence another person to change a behavior. For example:

"Mom, would you mind driving me over to the gym later today? I'd really appreciate it."

"Carlos, would you please turn down the music a little? I need to study."

The "polite request" concept may seem so simple that it sounds ridiculous, but it makes more sense if you consider how *im*polite we can be at times, especially when we're annoyed, stressed, or just in a hurry. For example:

"Mom, I need you to drive me to the gym." (No request, no "please," no appreciation; not likely to get good results.)

"Carlos! Turn down the #$%* music, will ya?!" (No comment.)

Sometimes the way we ask people for what we want is so disrespectful that it provokes an argument or some other negative response. Keeping it polite is not only more respectful, it's more effective.

When a polite request or suggestion doesn't work the first time, offer a friendly reminder:

"Mom, it's time to go to the gym."

"Carlos, please remember to turn down the music."

"i" messages

If the problem behavior continues despite your polite requests, you'll need a more assertive message. "I" messages are a firm and friendly communication that can produce surprisingly effective results. They're called "I" messages because they begin with the word "I".

An "I" message:

- allows you to say how you feel about the other person's behavior without blaming or labeling the person.

- makes it more likely that the other person will hear what you're saying because it's said in a respectful manner.

- tells the other person how the behavior is affecting you (your feelings).

- puts the emphasis on the other person's behavior rather than his or her personality.

- gives the other person clear information about what change in behavior you want.

how to send an "i" message

An "I" message works best when you deliver it with a firm, calm tone of voice. If you're angry, give yourself time to cool off before you approach the other person. An angry "I" message can escalate the situation into a full-fledged power struggle.

There are four steps to delivering an "I" message:

1. **Name the behavior or situation you want changed. Begin with, "I have a problem with..." or "When you...**

   "I have a problem with you yelling at me." or *"When you yell at me..."*

2. **Say how you feel without raising your voice.**

   "It feels like you don't respect me."

3. **State your reason.**

   "... because people don't usually yell at people they respect."

4. Say what you want done.

"I'd like you to talk to me calmly even when you're angry."

Putting the four steps all together, we have:

"I have a problem with you yelling at me. It feels like you don't respect me because people don't usually yell at people they respect. I'd like you to talk to me calmly, even when you're angry."

firm reminders

Changing habits and behavior isn't easy, whether it's your own behavior or someone else's. If an "I" message doesn't get the result you wanted, and the behavior continues, your next step is to give a short but firm reminder.

Self-discipline example (to influence yourself to keep better track of your assignments):

Write it down!

Assertive example (to influence someone to speak calmly instead of yelling):

Don't yell.

Remember to make solid eye contact and speak firmly but calmly. If the other person complies with your request, build on this success by encouraging him with a simple, "Thanks. I appreciate it." Or in the case of self-discipline, encourage yourself! "Nice job, self. I appreciate it!"

"I" MESSAGE PRACTICE

If you're participating in a *Teens in Action* or *Families in Action* program, you'll be doing this activity with your group. Use the instructions for partners below.

Practice "I" messages by writing one for each of the following situations. Use words that you'd be comfortable saying.

To do this activity with a partner: After you write your "I" message, deliver it to your partner. Then your partner tells you what he or she heard in the "I" message, acknowledging (1) the behavior that is causing a problem, (2) his or her feelings about the situation, and (3) what you expect him or her to do in the future.

SITUATION #1

Your little sister left the caps off most of your markers. They dried out. Now you can't finish your science project on time. Give your sister an "I" message.

I have a problem with _____

_____ .

I feel _____

Because _____

_____ .

I would like _____

_____ .

SITUATION #2

Your parent makes a teasing remark about how fat you look in your new jeans. Give your parent an "I" message.

I have a problem with _____

_____ .

I feel _____

Because _____

_____ .

I would like _____

_____ .

SITUATION #3

Your best friend always talks about how great he is at doing everything. You're tired of hearing about it. Give your friend an "I" message.

I have a problem with _____

_____ .

I feel _____

Because _____

_____ .

I would like _____

_____ .

SITUATION #4

You have forgotten to do an important assignment …again. Give <u>yourself</u> an "I" message to help you remember next time.

I have a problem with _____

_____ .

I feel _____

Because _____

_____ .

I would like _____

_____ .

BASIC DISCIPLINE PRACTICE

If you're participating in a *Teens in Action* or *Families in Action* program, you'll be doing this activity with your group, but you can also complete it on your own.

Practice using the basic discipline methods again, this time with a real problem you're having with yourself or someone else

Write down the problem here: _____
_____
_____

Polite request: _____
_____
_____

"I" Message: _____
_____
_____
_____
_____

Firm Reminder: _____
_____
_____

This week, put your plan into action and use the statements you wrote above to actually address your problem. Remember, you don't necessarily have to use all three of them. Use only as much assertiveness as you need to get a positive result. Afterwards, complete the remaining questions:

How did your polite request, "I" message, and/or firm reminder work out? _____
_____
_____

What, if anything, would you do differently next time you use these methods? _____
_____
_____

LESSONS FROM THE *TITANIC*

CAPTAIN, I JUST RECEIVED THIS TELEGRAPH FROM SHORE. WE ARE HEADING INTO A DANGEROUS ICE FIELD. DO YOU WANT TO CUT OUR ENGINES AND CHANGE COURSE?

NO WAY, JOSÉ. WE'VE GOT A SPEED RECORD TO BREAK AND I AIM TO DO IT.

MY NAME IS CLIVE, AND THAT ICEBERG LOOKS AWFULLY LARGE AND POINTY, AND WE'RE GETTING VERY CLOSE TO IT.

WE'LL SURVIVE, CLIVE. WE CAN PROBABLY GET AROUND THAT BERG, AND IN ANY CASE, THIS SHIP IS UNSINKABLE, OR HAVEN'T YOU HEARD?

SEE, I TOLD YOU WE WOULD GET AROUND IT.

SCREEEEEEEEEECH!!!

THAT'S THE SOUND OF OUR HULL BEING RIPPED BENEATH THE WATER BY THE BOTTOM OF THE ICEBERG—YOU KNOW,

THE BIG PART!

WELL, THERE GOES THE SPEED RECORD, BUT AT LEAST WE'RE STILL UNSINKABLE.

Written by Michael H. Popkin. Art by Juan Chavarriga.

CONSEQUENCES

Sometimes people won't change their behavior even when you've used polite requests, "I" messages, and firm reminders. In these cases, you can turn to more **advanced discipline methods**:

- Natural and logical consequences (covered in this chapter)
- The FLAC Method (covered in Chapter 4)

Remember that a key aspect of responsibility is accepting that what happens to us is a result of our choices.

R = C + C
Responsibility = Choice + Consequences

It stands to reason, then, that to teach yourself responsibility, you need to be able to connect each choice you make to the consequences you experience from it. We can learn a lot about what works and what doesn't from the consequences of our actions. Your parents and other adults can use these methods to help you learn responsibility and good decision-making; you can use them with others and yourself to help change behavior. There are two basic types of consequences: natural and logical.

natural consequences

Natural consequences "just happen" as the result of behavior. They happen without parents, teachers, other adults, or anyone else having to be involved.

> **Natural consequences:**
>
> The results that occur from a teen's behavior without
>
> any interference by a parent or other person

For example…

- The natural consequence of not putting gas in the car is running out of gas.
- The natural consequence of staying up really late on a school night is being tired at school the next day.
- The natural consequence of leaving a bicycle outside may be that it gets rusty or that it's stolen.

Natural consequences are powerful teachers. We've all learned important life lessons from the consequences of our own direct experience without parents or others intervening in any way. But natural consequences aren't good for teaching in every situation. There are three circumstances in which we shouldn't allow things to "just happen."

When the situation is too dangerous

The natural consequence of experimenting with drugs can be addiction or even death.

When the consequence is too far in the future

If someone tells you, "If you don't study for your algebra test, you won't get into the college you want," you probably aren't going to believe it. One test in middle school isn't going to have an effect on which college you attend.

When the consequence affects someone else more than it affects you

You borrow your mom's car and return it with the gas gauge on empty, so your mom runs out of gas.

logical consequences

When parents want their teen to change a behavior and they can't rely on natural consequences to help, we encourage them to work with the teen to set *logical consequences*.

> **Logical consequences:**
> Discipline that is logically connected to a misbehavior
> and is applied by an authority figure to influence someone
> to behave within the limits of a situation

Examples of parents using logical consequences with teens:

When Sean keeps forgetting to bring his dirty dishes into the kitchen after snacking in the den, he loses the privilege of taking food out of the kitchen.

If Susan forgets to put gas in Mom's car when she borrows it, she's not allowed to use the car for a week.

Teens can use logical consequences to influence themselves and others to change an unwanted behavior.

Examples of teens using logical consequences with other teens:

When Juan continues to yell at Carlos, Carlos stops hanging out with him.

When Janelle continues to bring alcohol to parties, she stops getting invited to parties.

Examples of teens using logical consequences with themselves:

When Clay realizes he needs help remembering to do his assignments, he decides that he won't watch TV or play video games until he has completed all his work for that day.

When Shauna realizes that she still has a problem smoking, she decides that she'll either quit on her own by the end of the month or she'll enter a quit smoking program.

Logical consequences aren't the same thing as punishment. Some of the differences are:

LOGICAL CONSEQUENCES VS. PUNISHMENT

LOGICAL CONSEQUENCES	PUNISHMENT
Logically connected to the misbehavior	Not connected to the misbehavior
Delivered in a firm and calm way	Often delivered with anger or resentment
Respectful	Disrespectful
Democratic: allows the teen to participate	Dictated by authority

logical consequences guidelines

Many people unintentionally turn a would-be logical consequence into a punishment, and then they wonder why the other person responds with anger, rebellion, or a power struggle. A few basic guidelines will help you develop fair and effective logical consequences.

GUIDELINES FOR USING LOGICAL CONSEQUENCES

1. Work together to help decide the consequence.

2. Put the consequence in the form of a choice:
   - either/or choice
   - when/then choice

3. Make sure the consequence is logically connected to the misbehavior.

4. Keep your tone of voice firm and calm.

5. Be willing and able to enforce the consequence.

choices, choices!

Logical consequences teach responsibility, which means "choices plus consequences;" therefore, always present your consequence in the form of a choice. The other person can choose positive behavior with a naturally-occurring positive consequence, or she can choose to continue the negative behavior and have you provide a logical consequence.

Try one of these types of choices:

- Either/or choices: "Either _____ or _____. You decide."

- When/then choices: "When you have _____, then you may _____."

Either/or choices are best used when you want to influence someone to <u>stop</u> a behavior. Remember to follow the guidelines of logical consequences. Examples of either/or choices:

Parent problem: Katherine leaves her stuff scattered around the den in the afternoon.

"Katherine, either put your things away when you come home from school, or I'll put them in a box in the basement. You decide."

Teen problem: Cal's friend, Austin, has asked him for help with his homework, but what he seems to really want is for Cal to do it for him.

"Austin, either stop fooling around and try to understand this stuff or I'm going to go home and work on my own. You decide."

Self problem: Austin is having trouble focusing on his homework.

"When Cal comes over to help me this afternoon, I can either pay attention and really work at getting it or I'll have to pay a tutor to help me later."

When/then choices are best used when you want to influence yourself or another to <u>start</u> a positive behavior. They take two events and order them so that the person must do what she likes doing least before she's allowed to do what she prefers. This isn't a bribe or reward, because both behaviors are a normal part of the teen's life already. Examples of when/then choices:

Parent problem: Selina has trouble getting her homework done but likes to surf the Internet.

Parent: *"Selina, when you've finished your homework, then you may get on the Internet."*

Teen problem: Sara's friend, Michael, has been treating her disrespectfully lately. She likes him otherwise, but she doesn't want to tolerate his put-downs any longer.

Sara: *"When you decide to start treating me respectfully again, text me.. But until then, forget my number."*

Self problem: I need to fulfill my responsibilities, but there are so many fun things I'd rather be doing.

"When I've worked out for thirty minutes, then I'll play some of my video game."

"When I finish reading this assignment, then I'll text my friend."

USING LOGICAL CONSEQUENCES

Describe a problem you're having with another person or with yourself.

_____

_____

Write a logical consequence you could set to prevent the problem from occurring again.

_____

_____

What words will you use to present the logical consequence? Write a sentence or two.

_____

_____

AFTER YOU PRESENT THE LOGICAL CONSEQUENCE:

What was the other person's response to the logical consequence? Did he or she test you to see if you would follow through?

_____

_____

If the consequence isn't working, do you think you need to stick with it longer or change the consequence to something else?

_____

_____

If the consequence isn't working, have you violated any of the guidelines for setting up logical consequences?

_____

_____

What do you like about the way you handled the use of logical consequences?

_____

_____

What will you do differently next time?

_____

_____

IDEAS FOR LOGICAL CONSEQUENCES

If your parents are taking a *Families in Action* course with you, you'll be using this activity to practice working together to set logical consequences.

Coming up with good logical consequences requires practice and creativity. For each of the problems below, put yourself in the parent's position and come up with some appropriate logical consequences to influence your teenager to stop the problem behavior. Remember to follow the logical consequences guidelines!

PROBLEM: **Playing video games at a time other than that agreed upon as "screen time"**

LOGICAL CONSEQUENCES:

(1) Losing telephone privileges for an evening (or a week, if this becomes a repeated infraction)

(2) _____
_____

(3) _____
_____

PROBLEM: **Coming home 20 minutes after curfew**

LOGICAL CONSEQUENCES:

(1) Having to come home 20 minutes before curfew next time, earlier if the problem continues.

(2) _____
_____

(3) _____
_____

PROBLEM: **Room is not clean when company is coming for the weekend.**

LOGICAL CONSEQUENCES:

(1) Cannot go out with friends until room is clean

(2) _____
_____

(3) _____
_____

Continued on next page

PROBLEM: Dinner dishes aren't washed by 8:00 p.m. as agreed upon.

LOGICAL CONSEQUENCES:

(1) Parent engages in "chore swapping" and does the dishes but then leaves teen's laundry for her to do for herself.

(2) _____

_____

(3) _____

_____

PROBLEM: Coat, books, and other items are left strewn from one end of the house to the other.

LOGICAL CONSEQUENCES:

(1) Items, except for schoolbooks, disappear for a pre-specified period of time.

(2) _____

_____

(3) _____

_____

Brainstorm a problem behavior and two logical consequences to go with it.

PROBLEM:

_____

_____

LOGICAL CONSEQUENCES:

(1) _____

_____

(2) _____

_____

FAMILY ENRICHMENT ACTIVITY: POSITIVE "I" MESSAGES

We learned earlier in this chapter that "I" messages offer an effective way to confront people about repeated problems. An "I" message can also be useful as an encouraging statement when someone successfully makes a change that you requested. *Positive "I" messages* can help motivate people to continue improving their behavior.

A positive "I" message has four steps that are similar but not identical to the steps of a regular "I" message:

1. **State what you like.**

   I really appreciate how you've stopped putting me down.

2. **Say how you feel.**

   I feel good around you again,

3. **Tell them why.**

   …because I can trust you not to hurt me.

4. **Offer to do something for them.**

   Do you want to do something together this weekend?

Don't worry if you don't use every step of the positive "I" message every time. The first step is encouraging by itself. And feel free to use your own words so that the message feels natural to you.

CHAPTER 3 HOME ACTIVITIES

1. Read Chapter 4 of this guide.

2. Practice using polite requests, "I" messages, and firm reminders. Complete the "Basic Discipline Practice" guide sheet on page 93.

3. Practice using a logical consequence to solve a problem you have with another person or with yourself. Complete the "Using Logical Consequences" guide sheet on page 102.

4. Practice coming up with logical consequences that are appropriate for different problem situations. Complete the "Ideas for Logical Consequences" guide sheet on pages 103-104.

5. Complete the "Teen Action Report" exercises on page 106.

TEEN ACTION REPORT

Write your responses to the following questions on a separate sheet of paper or in a journal.

about yourself

1. In what ways are you responsible? In what areas of your life do you think you should work towards taking more responsibility for yourself?

2. What's something you've learned through natural consequences?

3. What are some behaviors of yours that your parent(s) might think need to be met with logical consequences?

about your family

1. What are some areas of your family life that might be improved by developing and enforcing logical consequences?

2. What areas of your family life might be improved by providing positive feedback?

about your school

1. Are there any areas of your school life in which you need to become more responsible? What are they?

2. What are some areas of school life that might be improved by developing and enforcing logical consequences?

CHAPTER 4

BUILDING COURAGE AND SELF-ESTEEM

Matt, 15

Fifteen-year-old Matt had been having a very bad week. First, he got a "D" on his biology test. *Guess I should've studied,* he thought gloomily. To make matters worse, his younger sister Abby had come home with an "A" on her civics quiz. The way his parents were gushing over her was enough to make him sick. He retreated to his room, stuck in his earbuds, and cranked the music up, and now he was staring moodily into the mirror. Yep, breaking out all over. *What a loser. Well, at least I have a good body,* he told himself as he flexed a muscle. *Isn't that something girls are supposed to be into?* Then his heart sank as he remembered the ragging he'd gotten from his best friend, Steve. "If you leave tenth grade still a virgin, I'm gonna kick your butt." Steve had had sex for the first time in eighth grade. He had a lot of confidence around girls. *Which, of course, I don't.* Matt thought about the party coming up on Saturday night. *Maybe that's when it can happen with Julie.* After all, this would be their third date. A lot of guys Matt knew—Steve among them—only needed a couple of hours with a girl to score. *Maybe if I can get her to down a couple of drinks....*

COURAGE: ONE FROM THE HEART

The teen years are a time of ups and downs, stress, and discouragement. Very few people make it through painlessly. It can be tough keeping spirits up when it seems like the world is intent on bringing you down. Sometimes it's tempting to grasp at low-hanging values—anything to feel better. It takes courage to hold out for the "higher" values, to hang in there and keep trying when self-doubt grips the heart and twists. In the story you've just read, Matt lacks that courage. In other words, he's become **dis**-couraged. Matt has lost heart.

We learned earlier that the French word *coeur*, meaning "heart," is the base of the English word *courage*. Just as the heart has long been considered a symbol for the center of human emotions, courage might be thought of as the core of a person's character.

Courage is linked to fear. This is especially evident during times of risk. *Do I go ahead or turn back? What if I fail? What if they reject me? Do I dare to take the chance?* It's our courage that keeps us going when the easier path is to quit or give in to an unwise temptation. Because striving for most positive goals in life requires some risk, courage is essential. To become responsible, you have to risk the consequences of your choices. To cooperate with others, you have to risk that they may take advantage of you. Honesty, hard work, and even love all require some risk.

COURAGE IS THE CONFIDENCE TO TAKE A KNOWN RISK FOR A KNOWN PURPOSE.

If you don't know the consequences of a risk you decide to take, then the act isn't courageous; it's foolish and reckless. For example, if you take drugs for the thrill of it, thinking nothing bad will happen to you, that's not being courageous. You don't know the real risks. Contrast this with the teen who makes an "F" on a test but decides to study for hours to do better on the next one. He's showing a lot of courage, a lot of character.

Courage and Fear

Courage and Fear

Courage first met Fear
When I was still a child;
Courage gazed with cool, clear eyes;
Fear was something wild.

Courage urged "Let's go ahead;"
Fear said "Let's turn back."
Courage spoke of what we had,
Fear of what we lacked.

Courage took me by the hand
And warmed my frozen bones;
Yet Fear the while tugged at my legs
And whispered "We're alone."

Many have been the obstacles
Since first I had to choose,
And sometimes when Courage led me on
I've come up with a bruise.

And many have been the challenges
Since Fear and Courage met,
And yet those times I've followed Fear,
Too often tagged along Regret.

-- Michael Popkin

SELF-ESTEEM: ONE FROM THE MIND

Courage comes from a belief in yourself: that regardless of any particular outcome, you are a lovable, capable, giving person who has a good chance to succeed. And when you don't succeed, you look inward for a belief that you are more than just your achievements, that there is something worthwhile about you just because you are yourself. This belief—your *self-esteem*—helps motivate you to continue to work hard for good grades even after you've received a low one. It gives you the confidence to say "no" to friends when they want you to do things you know you should stay away from, even when they invite you to use drugs or engage in other destructive behavior.

When self-esteem is high—when we think we have a reasonable chance to succeed but all is not lost if we don't—we have the confidence to tackle life's challenges. We have courage.

High Self-esteem ⟹ *Courage*

Teens with high self-esteem have the courage to take positive risks. They are more likely to:

- risk making mistakes in school by tackling hard problems and trying their best.

- do what they know is right even if they lose their friends in the process.

- cooperate with others for the greater good even when they don't always get their way.

- find positive ways to achieve independence and challenge themselves.

Unfortunately, the opposite is also true. When we think of ourselves as unlovable or incapable of success, our self-esteem drops. This produces discouragement and fear.

Low Self-esteem ⟹ *Discouragement*

When teens suffer from low self-esteem, they may not bother taking risks at all, or they may become reckless and take unwise risks. They are more likely to:

- develop an "I don't care" attitude towards school and stop working or drop out.
- change their values to conform to those of their peers.
- resent authority and rebel, either openly or passively, through intentional failure and other means.

- resort to negative behavior—often involving drugs, sexuality, and violence—to achieve independence and challenge themselves.

self-esteem, courage, and body image

Let's face it. Our society puts way too much emphasis on looks. As a result, teens' self-esteem is often attached to how attractive they think they are. Considering that the people they compare themselves to are often impossibly perfect, this puts teens in a no-win situation. Everywhere we look—on billboards, in magazines, on TV—we see models whose primary function is to be beautiful and sexy. Their photos are often altered to create unrealistic perfection: inches are shaved off; skin tone smoothed out; legs made longer; muscle tone added. Supermodels often lead extreme lifestyles to support their body image, including drug use, surgery, and unhealthy dieting.

At an age when girls are naturally putting on fat and are going through other hormonal changes, they're bombarded with images of women too thin to menstruate. Most adults realize that these are not realistic images of women, but many teen girls don't know that. Little wonder that so many become bulimic or anorexic in an attempt to stay thin. Teenage boys are not exempt. The media is full of idealized images of men with sculpted bodies that are often only attainable through surgery, steroid use, or a ridiculous amount of time in a gym. We're seeing more and more incidents of eating disorders among boys and young men.

Bottom line: Get in shape because it's good for you, not because you want to look like the media's ideal of beauty. You'll have more energy and be healthier in general. Take care of your personal grooming, and choose your clothing to express yourself for the situations you're in. Sure, these things will also make you look better. Looking good is OK, but be wary of overemphasizing the looks. There are more important things to focus on.

Interview with the Vampire with Low Self-Esteem

As a former psychotherapist I've had a few interesting encounters with some very special clients whose problems arose from... most unusual circumstances. And yet their problems were very human ones. These clients just needed a little help getting back on track.

One that I found particularly engaging was a young woman, or at least she appeared as such, who was having difficulty getting motivated...

Please, uh, have a seat. Would you like some water or- ahem-never mind.

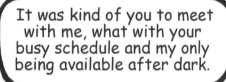

It was kind of you to meet with me, what with your busy schedule and my only being available after dark.

I'm happy to help, but I do have a ground rule: If you even look at my neck in a hungry sort of way, that's the end of your therapy.

Relax. You're not my type anyway.

And Ground Rule #2: No more old vampire jokes.

Sorry. I guess I can't do anything right.

Feeling a little down I see.

I guess.

How long?

400 years.

Hmmm. Tell me more.

It all began when I became a vampire back in the 17th century. I thought I was real cool at first. Super powers, immortality... who could want more?

SIGH!

But with time I've realized that I'm pretty much alone. I haven't met any other vampires that I trust, and human friends? Well, you can see the problem with that.

Everyone needs friends. I can see why you feel so sad.

And the villagers with their torches and pitchforks... They hate me! And I can hardly blame them. It's gotten to where I just stay in my cave and catch mosquitos. The best I can say for that is it passes the time.

But is there anything that makes you happy? Maybe a hobby, a skill, something you do well?

Well, I'm pretty good at flying. And I can vanish into thin air like nobody's business.

But really, what's the point when I have no one to share it with? I may as well just drive a stake through my own heart and be done with it.

I can see that you're really discouraged. But suicide, or whatever you call it when you're already dead, is never the answer. It's like missing the end of a movie. You don't get to see if it gets better. And it usually does, especially if you take action to make it better.

Action, huh? Like what?

I don't think you're going to like it.

Written by Michael H. Popkin. Art by Ron Wheeler.

ROUND AND ROUND: THE THINK-FEEL-DO CYCLE

Ever wonder why you feel the way you do about things? A lot of people think that the events in their life cause their feelings. For example, somebody says something mean to you and as a result, you feel bad. Makes sense, doesn't it? Fortunately, it isn't true. Events rarely cause feelings; rather, they trigger our belief systems, including all our attitudes and values. In other words, **events** trigger us to **think**, and it's this **thinking** that actually causes our **feelings**. Why is this fortunate? Because although we can't always control the events in our lives, we can control our thinking about those events.

Ever wonder why you **do** the things you do? It's connected to the way you **think** and **feel**. When an **event** occurs, your **thoughts** and **feelings** bat it back and forth as you work out how you can best achieve your goals in the current situation. You use all of this information to make a decision about what to **do**. Sometimes this happens so fast that you aren't even aware it's happening!

What you **do** then influences the next **event**, which then influences your thinking again, your feelings, and your next behavior. This can go round and round as long as you continue to engage the event.

We call this the Think-Feel-Do Cycle, and it looks like this:

The Think-Feel-Do Cycle

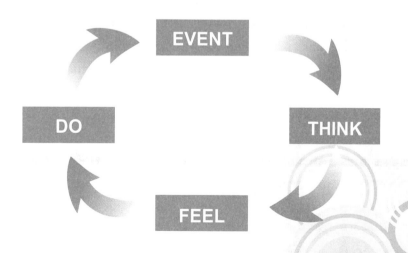

Here's an example. Shelly is a quiet fourteen-year-old who one day sees another girl sitting alone in the cafeteria (the Event). She thinks this looks like a good opportunity to make a friend (Think) and musters the courage (Feel) to ask the other girl if she can join her (Do). The girl responds positively (Event) and Shelly sits down. Before long they're talking about all kinds of things, and when lunch ends, Shelly had a good feeling inside. That afternoon, she finds herself more talkative than usual in class, and she carries her good feeling throughout the day. The next day at lunch she seeks out her new friend, and again they shared a pleasant meal, this time making plans to see a movie together over the weekend. Shelly's courage has been rewarded with a new friend, and she has moved into a success cycle where positive thoughts trigger positive feelings and behavior and lead to positive events and success.

Now let's see how the Think-Feel-Do Cycle reveals Matt's thought process from our opening story. The first event mentioned is that he got a "D" on his biology test. Matt's thinking about this event may have gone something like this:

Values: *"Doing well in school is important."*

Beliefs: *"I blew it. I knew I wasn't very smart. Abby's the smart one in the family. I'm pretty pathetic."*

These negative thoughts lowered Matt's self-esteem and triggered negative feelings, such as anger, sadness, and discouragement. These feelings led to more negative behavior on Matt's part.

Of course, there's always more than one event going on at a time in your life. Matt is being influenced by lots of events, such as his other school subjects, his family, friends, and social life. When more than one event at a time goes bad, the resulting stress is multiplied. This is what's happening to Matt as he thinks and feels about his acne, how he compares to his sister, his lack of sexual experience, and his upcoming date with Julie.

It takes courage to tolerate setbacks and disappointments. When courage is low, a teen may look for a quick way to reduce the pain. He could do this through a positive outlet like exercise, music, or talking to someone who cares. Unfortunately, teens sometimes turn to negative behavior to get some temporary relief. Let's see how this plays out in Matt's case.

When Matt finally got out of bed on Sunday, his head hurt...

Matt's Story, continued

When Matt finally got out of bed on Sunday, his head hurt and he had an empty feeling in the pit of his stomach. He cringed as the events of last night came back to him. *How could I have been so stupid?* Everything had been going great with Julie. Then he'd started drinking. Matt sat back down on the edge of the bed and tried to remember what happened next. Oh yeah. Steve had told him about the empty bedroom upstairs and had handed him a condom. *Why didn't I just laugh and walk away?*

He'd escorted Julie up there. They were laughing, and Matt made her a drink with the vodka he'd smuggled out of his house. But then he'd pulled out the condom and it was all downhill from there. Julie had said something like, "You've got to be kidding!" *That* wasn't part of the plan. He was a little fuzzy about what had happened next except that Julie was really mad–pushing him away and getting up to leave, and then he was alone. As these details came back to him, Matt put his head in his hands. *Just let me curl up and die.*

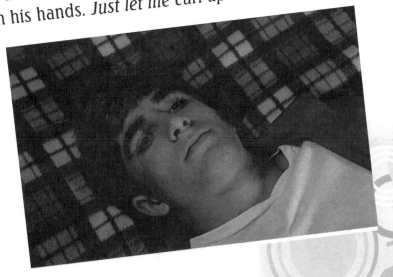

FAILURE AND SUCCESS CYCLES

When a teen reacts to events in his life with low self-esteem and a poorly developed system of values, the discouragement and negative behavior that follow usually produce more negative events. In Matt's case, these events might include getting dumped by Julie, increasing alcohol abuse, and more low grades at school. These kinds of events are likely to provoke harsh criticism and punishment from autocratic ("dictator") adults, which triggers more negative thinking and lower self-esteem, more discouragement, and more misbehavior and failure.

Failure Cycle

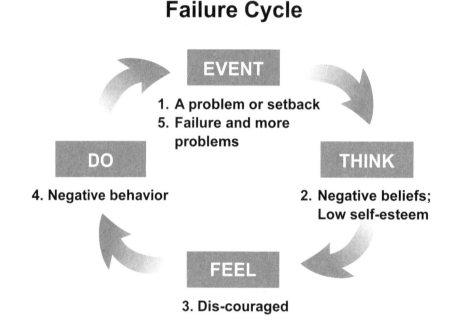

A teen with higher self-esteem than Matt's and more positive beliefs about himself might have responded very differently to the failed biology test. He may have thought, *I really blew it. I'll have to study big-time for the next test to make up for this.* Such thinking may have led to some feelings of remorse for the bad grade, but it would not have led to discouragement for this teen. In fact, a teen with high self-esteem and a well-developed set of values can take failure and turn it into a positive experience by learning from his mistakes. This positive behavior usually produces more successful events: better grades, positive feedback from adults, more privileges, etc. Successes like this strengthen the teen's self-esteem and courage, motivating him to keep trying for positive behavior, and so he sees more and more success. This is a **success cycle**, and though it may seem like a complex concept, we can sum it up in a few words: Nothing succeeds like success.

Julie is a good example of someone in a success cycle. Her high self-esteem and mature attitude about sexuality gave her the courage to resist Matt's advances. She took positive action to solve the problem by leaving. She'll feel good when she thinks about how she handled herself. Her self-esteem will strengthen, and she'll feel encouraged to stand up for herself the next time she's threatened.

Success Cycle

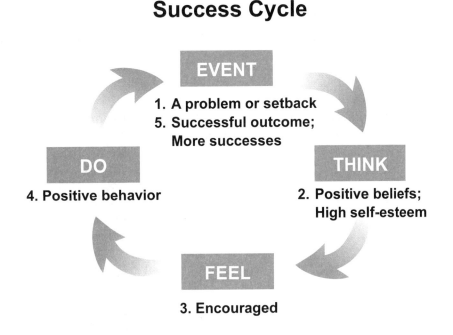

EVENT
1. A problem or setback
5. Successful outcome;
   More successes

THINK
2. Positive beliefs;
   High self-esteem

FEEL
3. Encouraged

DO
4. Positive behavior

Even if you think you're in a failure cycle, don't give up hope! You can decide to change direction at any time. We all have opportunities to choose what we do and how we think about ourselves and our lives. Sometimes you just need to identify one positive quality or event in your life to kick-start a success cycle. For example, working on a new talent or skill can bring out the best in you. Or, if you're feeling too discouraged to take that first step, seek out a friend who can encourage you or an adult you can talk to. Introduce just one positive choice into your life, and before you know it, the failure cycle is broken and a success cycle has begun!

SUCCESS OR FAILURE? THE CHOICE IS YOURS

If you're using this guide as part of the *Teens in Action* or *Families in Action* program, you'll be completing the following exercise with your group, but you may also complete it on your own.

The following example shows how a single event can be the start of either a failure cycle or a success cycle. What you think, feel, and do about the event determines which direction it goes.

EVENT

I saw the girl/boy I like standing by another girl's/boy's locker and laughing together. They seemed to be standing pretty close to each other.

FAILURE CYCLE	SUCCESS CYCLE
THINK NEGATIVELY	**THINK POSITIVELY**
I can't believe s/he's talking to that jerk. I won't put up with this. S/he's gonna be sorry.	I'm glad my girlfriend/ boyfriend)has other friends s/he can talk to.
FEEL NEGATIVELY	**FEEL POSITIVELY**
I must be a real loser for my girlfriend/boyfriend to like (other person) more than s/he likes me. I feel hurt, angry, and **discouraged**, and I'm going to show them.	I'm proud to have a girlfriend/boyfriend who makes friends easily and is well liked. I feel happy for him/her and good about myself. It's **encouraging** to have such a cool girlfriend/ boyfriend.
DO NEGATIVELY	**DO POSITIVELY**
I walk up to the two of them and glare. When they ask me what's wrong I say, "What do you think is wrong?" Then I take my girlfriend's/boyfriend's arm and say, "Let's go." and I pull him/her down the hall to our next class.	I walk up to them and say, "Hey!" I ask the other person how s/he's doing, make a positive comment, and then ask my girlfriend/ boyfriend if s/he wants to hang out after school.
NEGATIVE RESULT (EVENT)	**POSITIVE RESULT (EVENT)**
My girlfriend/boyfriend pulls away from me and says, "I don't know what your problem is, but leave me alone." I walk away angrier than ever, feeling like a total loser and wanting to get even with both of them.	Both of them say, "Hey" back. We talk for a minute. My girlfriend/boyfriend agrees to meet up at 3:00. I walk away feeling really good about us. I can tell s/he's feeling good about us, too.

Continued on next page

Now try this exercise with an event from your own life. Think of a recent event or situation that had a negative impact on you or led you to respond negatively. It can be as simple as a hurtful remark that someone made or as major as a break-up with a favorite boy- or girlfriend. Once you come up with an event, **follow the instructions in green** to complete the chart below.

EVENT	
Write a brief description of your event.	
FAILURE CYCLE	**SUCCESS CYCLE**
THINK NEGATIVELY	**THINK POSITIVELY**
Write some negative thoughts you had about the event.	Write the positive thoughts that you could have had.
FEEL NEGATIVELY	**FEEL POSITIVELY**
Write the negative feelings you had in response to your negative thoughts.	Write the positive feelings you would have had in response to the thoughts you wrote above.
DO NEGATIVELY	**DO POSITIVELY**
Write the negative action or behavior you took in response to the negative feelings.	Write the positive action you would have taken in response to more positive thoughts.
NEGATIVE RESULT (EVENT)	**POSITIVE RESULT (EVENT)**
Write the negative results of your choices.	Write the positive results of your choices.

*The "Negative Result" or "Positive Result" becomes the next "Event" in your life. A negative event is likely to lead to more negative thoughts (discouragement) and lead you further into a failure cycle. A positive event will lead to greater self-esteem and the likelihood that you will be in a success cycle.

Continued on next page

Remember, you ALWAYS have a choice! You can choose the positive approach or the negative approach! (Warning: We aren't saying that you should never experience painful emotions like sadness or anger. Even in a success cycle, those feelings are sometimes necessary. What's important is whether these painful feelings get better or worse over time. How you choose to think and act will determine this.)

OK, so one thing you can do (or help someone do) to get out of failure cycles and into success cycles is to focus on the thinking and doing involved. As we've just seen, this involves positive thinking and focusing on solutions. Also, when someone is discouraged and falling into a failure cycle, what they may need most is encouragement.

Encouragement enters the Think-Feel-Do Cycle in the "Event" step. Encouraging events can come from parents and other adults, friends and other peers, or even from oneself. Encouragement is a skill, and it can be improved with good information and practice. So, let's look more closely at developing encouragement skills.

four ways you can be discouraging

Encouragement always begins with the same first step: recognizing and avoiding ways that you may be *dis*couraging.

***en*courage = "to give courage"**

***dis*courage = "to remove courage"**

Your words, thoughts, and actions are very powerful events in your own life as well as in other people's lives (including your parents!). Learning to avoid these four common ways we sometimes discourage will not only improve your relationships with others, it will help you feel better about yourself, too.

1. FOCUSING ON MISTAKES AND WEAKNESSES

We all make mistakes and have our weaknesses, and recognizing them is a good way to correct them and improve. But when someone is constantly pointing out your weak points, it can be hard on your self-esteem. This is particularly true if that someone is important to you, like a friend, a family member, or even yourself. Everyone is sensitive to criticism, so be careful about the feelings of others when you point out a problem. And when you catch your own mistakes and notice areas where you need to improve, learn to do it with a smile instead of a kick.

2. EXPECTING THE WORST OR TOO LITTLE

It feels pretty awful when someone doesn't believe in your abilities. If you don't believe in your own abilities, it might not only discourage you; it may hold you back. Everyone can improve. So, even in areas of weakness, focus on what can be done to get better rather than just lowering your expectations.

3. EXPECTING TOO MUCH (PERFECTIONISM)

On the other hand, if you expect more from yourself and others than is reasonable, it can become discouraging, as well. When someone you respect is never satisfied with your performance, when they get frustrated and angry at your mistakes, you may become anxious and make more mistakes, or you may stop trying altogether. Perfectionists are hard to be around, and even when they succeed, they take little satisfaction in it.

breaking from gender stereotypes

What kind of man or woman you become no longer has to be dictated by cultural stereotypes. Girls no longer have to be made of "sugar and spice and everything nice." Boys are able to choose from a lot more than just "frogs and snails and puppy dog tails." In other words, you're free to be you! In fact, the best You probably includes qualities that were once considered the sole property of the opposite sex. Here are some ideas for expanding beyond those old stereotypes.

- Value your skills and those of others, especially academic abilities.
- Value relationships as much as you do achievements.
- Appreciate qualities like courage, responsibility, respect, and caring in yourself and others.
- Support others, but also be assertive about what you want and need.
- Play sports and get involved in other healthy physical activities.
- Set long-term goals for yourself, which may or may not include marriage and a family.
- Discuss with others what you need to do to reach these goals.
- Participate in the arts and express yourself through drawing, writing, music, etc.
- When you think about career options, don't disregard those that are traditionally dominated by the opposite sex.
- Don't get your self-esteem from looks or from sex. Get it from your thoughts, feelings, and behavior.
- Respect others as equals. Don't judge them based on their looks.

4. OVERPROTECTING AND PAMPERING

If you're constantly avoiding reasonable risks and hard work, allowing others to step in and protect you from the consequences of your poor choices, you rob yourself of the opportunity to learn from experience. You may convince yourself that you aren't capable of handling things for yourself. It's OK to accept help from others, but it's not OK to let them take over for you. The same goes for when you're doing the helping: It's great to offer your help on a difficult task, but you aren't doing anyone a favor if you take over and do all the hard work.

Some parents act more like personal servants than parents, feeling they must protect their teens from life's harsh realities. Teens brought up this way form unrealistic ideas about how the world works. As they approach adulthood, they may not develop the motivation they need to do things for themselves. When things don't come easily to them, they become frustrated and angry. If you have overprotective parents, let them know that you appreciate their efforts, but you want to take over more responsibility for yourself. It takes courage to cut some strings, but in time you'll gain far more than you lose.

One more thing about parents: If yours do things to discourage you, you can try to encourage them to change, but you may not be successful. You can't control a lot of the events in your life, but you can control what you think about those events. You can choose not to let the words or actions of others discourage you. As Eleanor Roosevelt, one of America's greatest First Ladies, once said:

No one can make you feel inferior without your consent.

TURNING DISCOURAGEMENT INTO ENCOURAGEMENT

Fortunately, each of the four methods of discouragement can be turned around:

TURN DISCOURAGEMENT INTO ENCOURAGEMENT

Focus on mistakes and weaknesses ➡	Build on strengths
Expect the worst or too little ➡	Show confidence
Expect too much (perfectionism) ➡	Value the person as-is
Overprotect and pamper ➡	Spur independence

These methods of encouragement will work for all kinds of people, and even for yourself. After all, who doesn't need an occasional boost of self-esteem and courage? Let's look at the four methods more closely.

1. INSTEAD OF FOCUSING ON WEAKNESSES... BUILD ON STRENGTHS.

If you want to encourage someone to do better, find something you like about that person. This works when you want to help yourself do better, as well. When you focus on strengths rather than weaknesses, you build self-esteem and courage, and next comes positive behavior. You can also help improve a specific skill, value, or character trait. Plus, when you build on another person's strength, you'll strengthen your relationship with that person.

"You have a great sense of humor."

"Even though we argue a lot, I really admire how you stand up for yourself."

"I'm very organized, and I have a good memory. That can help in a lot of situations."

To help you effectively build on strengths, remember this: *Building on strengths is like putting money in the bank.* Just as a bank is a place where resources are invested for growth, you can use the BANK method to help yourself and others build personal assets and grow into a more successful human being. The four letters stand for:

Break it down into Baby steps.

Acknowledge strengths.

Nudge to take the next step.

Keep encouraging!

Break it down into Baby steps. Remember, you didn't learn to walk all at once. You learned step by step. When you break a goal into small, easy steps, success at each step feels encouraging and it motivates you to go for the next step. Keep going, and you'll reach your ultimate goal. This systematic approach can work for any skill, value, or character trait you want to build.

"I know school can be difficult, but if I break each assignment down into small steps I can do it."

"If you want to go out with Jess, the first step is to get to know her better. Let's focus on that."

Acknowledge what you can do well. Once you've identified a goal, get an idea where you are on the path towards reaching it. Knowing what you can already do will build confidence and motivation to take the next step.

"This isn't so bad. I already take good notes in my classes, and I block out time every night to do homework. I've got a pretty good start."

"You've got a great sense of humor. People like that about you. So when you text Jess, think of something funny to say."

Nudge yourself to take the next step. Learning requires risk, because with each new step, there's the potential for failure. Even if you have high self-esteem, fear of failure can make it difficult to take the next step. Mistakes or slow progress can often undermine courage and tempt you to give up. This is when an encouraging nudge can help give you enough courage to take the next step.

> *"I'm not doing as well as I hoped in algebra, but if I just stick with it a little longer, I know I'll get it! Maybe my next step should be to ask a good math student for help."*

> *"OK, so Jess didn't think that text joke was all that funny. But at least she knows you have the guts to tell a joke—and not everyone does. So, what's the next step? Maybe talk to her today at lunch?"*

Keep encouraging improvement and effort. Most people don't offer encouragement until they've achieved their ultimate goal. But that's a mistake. It's much more effective to offer encouragement at each step along the way. Any improvement is movement in the right direction and should be noticed and acknowledged. Success is a great motivator, so why not experience numerous successes along the way? This builds self-esteem and keeps you moving towards the goal. If you fall back a step (and that's to be expected), encouragement can help you keep at it and not give up. In fact, effort alone, even when not making progress, should always be encouraged.

> *"I'm getting better at finishing my homework assignments. One more day and I'll have made it through a whole week without giving up on an assignment!"*

> *"Hey, I saw you and Jess talking at lunch. Way to go!"*

2. INSTEAD OF EXPECTING THE WORST... SHOW CONFIDENCE.

To turn the discouraging practice of expecting the worst into encouragement, try showing confidence in yourself and in others instead. We build self-esteem and courage by developing skills and learning how to handle problems. But to do this, we need self-esteem and courage. It's a "chicken and egg" sort of situation. To make progress, you need to add a new factor: responsibility. By taking on new responsibilities and sticking with them even when the going gets tough, we build a foundation on which confidence can grow.

Taking on New Responsibilities: Accepting responsibility is a nonverbal way of showing confidence. It says, "I know you can do this."

"Hey, Mom. I know how busy you are now. Would it be a help if I took over cooking dinner one night a week?"

"I really like the videos you've been making. Would you be willing to do one to help us promote the concert next month?"

Sticking With It: When you refuse to give up easily, you're showing confidence in your ability to eventually succeed. When you encourage others to hang in there and keep working, you may be the difference between success or failure. Often the problems that are the hardest to solve are the ones that give the biggest boost to our courage and self-esteem when we finally triumph.

"I'm going to keep trying. I can do it!"

"I know this is hard, but if you keep practicing, you'll get it."

3. VALUE YOURSELF AS YOU ARE.

Self-esteem doesn't come from achievements alone. More important is that we feel accepted by significant people in our life. In fact, this is what most people want most: to be accepted for who they really are, not just for what they've accomplished. All people have the ability to learn from their mistakes and improve, but it's important for each of us to know that we are valuable as we are right now; that right now, we are already good enough.

There are some things you can do to communicate that you value yourself and others:

Separate the deed from the doer. When you mess up, focus your attention on your behavior, not your personality.

FOCUS ON THE DEED:	*"I shouldn't have said that. It was rude."*
NOT THE DOER:	*"I'm such a jerk! I can't do anything right."*
FOCUS ON THE DEED:	*"I failed the test because I didn't study enough."*
NOT THE DOER:	*"I failed the test because I'm stupid."*

You can also help others learn to separate actions from self-worth by gently correcting them when they get down on themselves.

Missing two foul shots doesn't make you a loser. It happens to the best players, too."

"You're not stupid. You made a mistake. We all do sometimes. You can do better next time."

Appreciate your uniqueness. Although we live in a society of equals, that doesn't mean we're all the same. It's important for each of us to know that we're one-of-a-kind, with unique dreams and talents. You can appreciate your own uniqueness by taking time to notice these things. You can show others that you appreciate the special things about them that make them unique, too.

"What do you dream about doing someday?"

"You have a great laugh."

"I like you."

"I love you."

4. INSTEAD OF OVERPROTECTION AND PAMPERING… SPUR INDEPENDENCE.

One of the goals of adolescence is to eventually break away from your parents and become an independent adult. This doesn't happen overnight. You still depend on your parents and other adults for many things, like food, clothing, and shelter. You also depend on them for help learning the rules of society, how to handle problems, and to help guide you in developing a strong character. The give and take of moving from total dependence on a parent (think "baby") to becoming an independent adult with all the freedoms that entails (think "21") is not just about age. It's about taking on more and more responsibility as you learn to stand on your own two feet. And just as a one-year-old feels the thrill of encouragement when she literally stands on her own two feet, every step you take in that direction also boosts your courage and self-esteem.

"I'd like to go to this camp for two weeks. Maybe I could pay for part and you could help with part. What do you think?"

"I won't switch the TV to the game console for you anymore, but I will be glad to teach you how to do it for yourself."

Take reasonable risks. Remember that courage is about having the confidence to take reasonable risks. But you need to find a balance between too much risk and too little. In the "too much" category, reckless risk-taking is almost guaranteed to put you in danger or land you in trouble. If you tend to be overly adventurous, consider reigning yourself in a little. If you're more on the "too little" side—overly cautious—look for opportunities to take more risks. It may help to talk with both peers and adults to get a feel for what others think are reasonable risks. Then be sure to talk to your parents to get permission and set guidelines before you take a risk.

"I'd really like to go to this concert. I have no problem with following the guidelines we've talked about."

"One of my teachers suggested that I try out for the school play. I'm kind of nervous about it, but I'd like to give it a try."

Life in a democratic society is neither independent nor dependent; we are all interdependent.

---

in·ter·de·pen·dent   *adjective*   /in-ter-di-pen-duhnt/

: relating to two or more things that are dependent on each other

---

Surviving and thriving in society, in your family, or in any group of people requires a willingness to depend on others and to allow them to depend on you. You can see interdependence in action all around you. For example:

- Playing on a sports team: You depend on your teammates to do their job, and they depend on you to do yours.

- Driving a car: You depend on other drivers to follow the traffic rules, and they depend on you to do the same.

- Living in a family: You depend on your parents and siblings for certain things, and they depend on you.

Remember, every new skill requires practice to get it right. The worksheets on the next few pages will help you learn to use your new encouragement skills.

ENCOURAGEMENT PROFILE

If you're participating in a *Teens in Action* or *Families in Action* program, you may be completing the following exercise with your group, but you can also do it on your own.

Before you can encourage someone—even yourself—you need to know what positive qualities, skills, and talents the person has. Fill in the blanks below to describe the strengths that both you and your parents bring to your family.

1. _____ does well at _____.
   (Mom, Dad, Stepmom, Stepdad, etc.)

   I do well at _____.

2. _____ helps me with _____.

   I help _____ with _____.

3. _____ is learning _____.

   I am learning _____.

4. A strength that _____ has is _____.

   One of my strengths is _____.

5. _____ can _____.

   I can _____.

6. _____ learned how to _____.

   I learned how to _____.

7. What I like best about _____ is _____.

   What I like best about myself is _____.

ENCOURAGING EACH OTHER

Write an encouraging response that you could give the person identified in each of the following situations.

1. Your friend Carol is upset because she found out that she didn't pass History, and now she'll have to go to summer school or repeat the class next year. She's afraid of how her parents are going to react. Encourage her.

2. Your friend Brandon has had a crush on a girl in your class all year. He finally got up the courage to ask her to the homecoming dance. Although she was nice about it, she said no. Encourage him.

3. You made the team (basketball, track, cheerleading, etc.) but your best friend, Chantelle, who also tried out, did not. Encourage her.

4. Most of the kids in your class have the newest style of shoes. You just got a new pair yourself. Your friend Ryan's parents won't let him get them because they say they're too expensive. Ryan feels discouraged about this. Encourage him.

ENCOURAGING YOURSELF

Practice the four methods of building encouragement in <u>yourself</u>.

SPUR YOUR INDEPENDENCE.

Think of three tasks that someone else is currently doing for you that you could do for yourself.

1. _____

2. _____

3. _____

Now choose one of these tasks to do for yourself this week. Don't forget to encourage yourself!

BUILD ON YOUR STRENGTHS.

Identify a goal and use the BANK method to help achieve it.

Goal: _____

Baby steps: Break the process of achieving your goal into three steps. 1. _____ 2. _____ 3. _____	**A**cknowledge what you already do well that will help you achieve the goal. _____ _____ _____
Nudge yourself to take the next step. What can you say to do this in an encouraging way? _____ _____ _____	**K**eep encouraging improvement. What words of encouragement can you use? _____ _____ _____

Continued on next page

ENCOURAGING YOURSELF

SHOW CONFIDENCE IN YOURSELF.

Accept at least one new responsibility this week and stick with it. Answer the questions below.

What new responsibility did you give yourself?

_____

When and how did you avoid the temptation to give up on the new responsibility?

_____

VALUE YOURSELF AS-IS.

Describe one way that you separated your worth from your accomplishments or mistakes this week.

_____

Describe at least one way that you appreciated your own uniqueness.?

_____

DON'T FIGHT. NEGOTIATE.

Most successful people, from world leaders to high school students, have learned that very few situations can be improved by fighting. Most conflicts are better resolved through *negotiation*.

> **ne•go•ti•ate** *verb* /ni-goh-shee-ayt/
>
> : to discuss with others in order to reach an agreement

Negotiating well takes some skill, and for that you need practice. But there are three things you can do right now that will help you be a successful negotiator.

1. **Calm down. Cool down. Collect yourself.**

   You can't solve problems effectively when you or the other person is angry or extremely anxious. So before you start, calm down and try to calm the other person down. If you can't, separate until later when you've both cooled off. (More on anger management coming up!)

2. **Make the *problem* the enemy, not the other person.**

   Focus on solving the problem, not on showing that you're the boss. The more egos get in the way, the less chance you have of finding a solution that all can live with.

3. **Use the FLAC Method to solve the problem.**

   The *what*? You may remember that we mentioned the FLAC Method in Chapter 3 as one of the advanced discipline methods. Let's see what it's all about…

using the FLAC method to solve a problem

The FLAC Method combines four skills into one powerful conflict-resolution tool. Each letter represents a skill:

Feelings

Limits

Alternatives

Consequences

You can use the FLAC Method to solve problems with your friends and other peers, with your parents and other adults, or even to solve your own problems.

Use it to negotiate with your parents when they have a problem with you. For example, your parents tell you they don't want you hanging around with your new friend, Devon.

Feelings: Use your listening and empathy skills to understand how the other person feels and what he or she wants.

"Let me see if I understand. You think that Devon is trouble, and you're worried that if I hang out with him, I'll get into trouble, too."

Limits: State your limits or the limits of the situation.

"I haven't gotten into trouble yet, and I don't plan on it. Hasn't my responsible behavior earned me the right to see who I want to see? Parents can't really choose their kids' friends, can they? I mean, did your parents choose your friends?"

Alternatives: Look for alternatives that work for both you and the other person.

"What if we agree that as long as I keep my grades up and don't get into any trouble, I can spend a reasonable amount of time with Devon?"

Consequences: Keep in mind the consequences of NOT solving the problem or keeping the agreement.

"If there are any problems, I'll stop meeting him."

Use it when you have a problem with a friend, a parent, a sibling, or anyone else. For example, a friend says to you, "Let's blow off school today."

F	*"Sounds like you're really up for an adventure,"*
L	*"…but that could get us into real trouble."*
A	*"Let's just plan to go to the skateboarding park on Saturday instead. We can't get busted for that."*
C	(If they pressure you to go): *"I told you, I'm not skipping school. Now either respect that or I won't be able to do anything Saturday either."*

Use it on yourself. For example, there's a party you want to go to, but you weren't invited…

F	*"I feel pretty hurt and angry because I really wanted to go."*
L	*"…but I wasn't invited, so that's not going to happen."*
A	*"I'd better find something fun to do that night. I'll find out who else wasn't invited and see if they want to do something."*
C	*"…or else I'll wind up sitting at home alone feeling sorry for myself."*

POWER THROUGH NEGOTIATION

Use the FLAC Method to negotiate a solution to a conflict you're having with a peer, your parents, or yourself. Answer the questions below to describe how it went.

Describe the problem:

_____

_____

Feelings: What did you say to acknowledge the person's feelings and goals?

_____

_____

Limits: What did you say to acknowledge the limits of the situation?

_____

_____

Alternatives: What alternatives did you and the other person come up with?

_____

_____

Consequences: If you decided on a consequence for breaking the agreement, what was it?

_____

_____

What would be the consequences of not coming up with a solution?

_____

_____

What did you like about how you handled the negotiation?

_____

What would you do differently next time?

_____

_____

HANDLING ANGER

One of the things that can get in the way of solving problems is anger. This is an emotion that has probably been around ever since a caveman on his way to pick some berries first discovered a fallen tree blocking his path.

A **little** anger can be good. It can help us get things done. Anger causes our bodies to release a chemical called *adrenaline*, which gives us extra strength and energy to accomplish physical tasks. Anger sends our brains a message: "Something is blocking one of our goals. Do something about it!" For the caveman, that something might have been to lift the tree and throw it aside with his adrenaline-powered super-strength. Problem solved. "Hmmm… anger good!"

Unfortunately, too much anger can cause all sorts of problems like physical violence, broken relationships, and crime. The key to managing anger is to respond to it before it gets too big. Learn to identify it when it's still small, then take appropriate action, and let it go. Don't ignore it until it overwhelms your thinking and makes a mess of things.

THREE TYPES OF ANGER

Passive Anger	Positive Anger	Over-the-top Anger
Ignores the problem May come out in stomach aches, headaches, passive-aggressive behavior	Lets us know there is a problem we need to solve Gives us energy and motivation	Used to intimidate others into giving us our way; alienates others; gets us in trouble

how to use anger positively

1. **Act early, before the anger escalates.** Ignoring anger usually just makes it grow bigger or come out at the wrong time, like with friends or through physical problems like stomach aches or trouble sleeping.

2. **Keep the anger under your own control.** When you allow others, your parents or peers included, to control your temper, you give away your power. Deep breathing, taking a time out, or other self-calming methods can help.

3. **Act to solve the problem that is frustrating you.** This is where the problem-handling skills we've been learning really come into play.

4. **Express your anger respectfully, with words.** If you're mad at another person, it can be a good first step to let him or her know you're angry without yelling or being insulting. Using the "I have a problem with…" or "I feel angry when…." from our "I" Messages skill is an excellent way to do that.

5. **Reduce the importance of your goal**—but first ask yourself what your goal is. Have you ever been angry at your parents for not letting you do something you wanted to do? Maybe the thing you're "dying to do" doesn't have to be as important as you make it. Maybe, if you keep control of your anger, you and your parents can find an alternative that will work for both of you.

PROBLEM-PREVENTION TALKS

Imagine how frustrating it would be to play a game of softball if you didn't know the rules. Rules are important for any sport or game, and the same goes for families. To prevent problems and get along well in a family, everyone needs to be clear about its rules and expectations. You all need to talk about the issues and scenarios that are most likely to lead to problems, and this needs to happen *before* the problems have the chance to occur. This kind of discussion is what we call a Problem-Prevention Talk.

Have you ever gotten in trouble for breaking a rule that you didn't know even existed? In the past you may have escaped any serious consequences by claiming ignorance, but as you get older and more independent, the price of not knowing a rule or ignoring it could be much higher than you want to pay. The issues most likely to cause problems in a teen's life, and therefore the ones you need to talk about with your family, are those that allow a new level independence, require responsibility, or might involve drug use, sexuality, or violence. For example:

PROBLEM-PREVENTION TALK TOPICS

- Schoolwork
- Use of the car
- Going to parties
- Choosing friends
- Handling anger

- Using the Internet
- Dating
- Spending the night out
- Curfews
- Household responsibilities (chores)

Talking about problems—even potential problems—with parents can be touchy. Anger may flare up on either side, and what started as a discussion can quickly turn into a power struggle. To keep a Problem-Prevention Talk civil, orderly, and democratic, we recommend that teens and parents use the following steps:

HAVING A PROBLEM-PREVENTION TALK

1. Identify potential problems and risks.

2. Share thoughts and feelings about these problems and acknowledge others' thoughts and feelings.

3. Generate guidelines through brainstorming and negotiation.

4. Decide on logical consequences for violating guidelines (if necessary).

5. Follow up later to make sure guidelines were followed and to enforce consequences (if necessary).

You may find that you don't need to follow these steps exactly, but it's a good idea to use them as guidelines. Let's go over them one by one.

1. Identify potential problems and risks.

At the start of the meeting, decide which potential problems you're going to discuss. Your parents may already have some topics in mind, but you can introduce issues that concern you, as well. For example:

Parents: *"You know how strongly we feel that you not smoke, drink, or use other drugs at parties. So, for us to feel good about you going to parties, we need to be clear about some things."*

Teen: *"OK. We can also talk about what you expect me to do if I go to a party and only then find out that people are drinking or doing drugs."*

2. Share thoughts and feelings.

Everyone who participates in a Problem-Prevention Talk gets an opportunity to share what he or she thinks about the situation and to express concerns.

Parents: *"We want to reduce the chance that someone pressures you to use drugs, which means not being around kids who are using them."*

Teen: *"OK, but I can't always know if someone is out in the car drinking or something."*

Parents: *"No, but you can tell if someone at the party is high on something."*

3. Generate guidelines through brainstorming and negotiation.

Keeping in mind the feelings and concerns that everyone shared in step two, talk about the expectations that should be set for the situation. While parents have the final word on this, teens should contribute, too. If parents set a guideline that a teen feels is so unfair that he or she is unlikely to follow it, it will do more harm than good. Often the best solutions are compromises between what the parents want and what the teen wants.

Parents: *"So, we agree that if anyone at the party is using alcohol or other drugs, you'll call us to pick you up."*

Teen: *"OK, but I'll be a lot more comfortable with this if you'd pick me up down the street from the party so that nobody will see me leaving with my parents."*

4. Decide on logical consequences for violating the guideline.

This step may not always be necessary, but setting a consequence for violating a guideline can work well for teens who need a little help staying on track. Teens and parents should work together to come up with appropriate consequences, if possible. This can help both sides get a better understanding of the other's priorities and concerns.

Parents: *"If you want to continue going to parties, you need to make sure you only stay if it's free of drugs and alcohol."*

Teen: *"OK."*

5. Follow up later.

When you make an effort to follow the rules, you generally want someone to know that you've done so. On the other hand, you may have run into a problem that prevented you from following a guideline that you and your parents set. In either case, it's a good idea for teens and parents to have a follow-up discussion after the teen has had the opportunity to test a guideline.

Parents: *"I spoke to Tracy's dad about the party last weekend. He said it went well, with no drinking or anything out of line."*

Teen: *"Yeah. His parents were keeping a good eye on things."*

HOME ACTIVITIES

1. Read Chapter 5 in this guide.

2. Practice using the Think-Feel-Do approach to change potentially negative events into positive ones. Complete the "Success or Failure: The Choice Is Yours" chart on page 123 to organize and track your progress.

3. Practice encouraging (and avoiding discouraging) yourself and others, using the four methods of encouragement. Complete the "Encouragement Profile," the "Encouraging Each Other" guide sheet, and the "Encouraging Yourself" guide sheet on pages 133-136.

4. Practice using the FLAC method to negotiate and solve problems. Complete the "Power through Negotiation" guide sheet on page 139.

5. Answer the "Teen Action Report" questions on page 145.

TEEN ACTION REPORT

Write your responses to the following questions on a separate sheet of paper or in a journal.

about yourself

1. What people and things discourage you? Encourage you? How can you spend more time and energy with encouraging people and activities?

2a. If you get angry about something that happens this week, practice using the Think-Feel-Do approach to create a better situation for yourself. Use the chart on the next page to track your progress.

What happened?	What did you decide to think?	How did you feel?	What did you do?	What were the consequences of what you did?	How did it affect your self-esteem?

2b. If you weren't satisfied with the outcome of any of the situations you wrote about in the chart above, how could you change either your thinking or what you did to create a better outcome?

about your family

1. What do you do to discourage other members of your family? What can you do to encourage them instead?

2. Practice using the FLAC Method to prevent a conflict from escalating at home this week. What was the conflict? How did you apply each of the four steps of the FLAC Method? What was the outcome?

about your school

1. In what ways do your friends at school encourage you and discourage you?

2. What kinds of things can you tell your friends to help them get into a success cycle or out of a failure cycle?

CHAPTER 5

DRUGS, SEXUALITY, AND VIOLENCE:

Reducing the Risks, Part 1

I can stop anytime I want, Kaitlyn told herself as she popped another couple of pills...

Kaitlyn

I can stop anytime I want, Kaitlyn told herself as she popped another couple of pills and swallowed them with a swig of beer. There's no way in #%$&* I'm ever getting addicted to anything. Three years later, after two interventions, two failed attempts at rehab, a few hospital visits, and several arrests, she did quit. In fact her life seemed to be back on track. She'd gone back to school to get her GED, and now she had plans to apply to colleges for the fall. That's why her family and friends were so surprised when they learned she had overdosed on heroin, and now Kaitlyn was dead.

On the same day that the local newspaper ran Kaitlyn's obituary it also carried a story about the 100th anniversary of the sinking of the Titanic: On April 10, 1912, the *Titanic* set off on its maiden voyage from England to New York. By all accounts, it was the safest ship ever built. Only five days after embarking, the captain received a telegram warning that a dangerous ice field lay ahead. He had plenty of time to slow the engines, change his course, and avoid risking a disaster. However, he mistakenly thought that he could save time by steering around any icebergs in his path. When a giant iceberg loomed ahead, he thought the ship could slide past. He did manage to steer around the portion of the iceberg that was visible above water, but not around the rest of it beneath the surface. It was this underwater portion that ripped through the Titanic's hull. The officer's mistake cost him his life as well as the lives of the 1,523 others who went down with the ship.

What do these two stories have in common? (Hint: Think of Kaitlyn as a teenage *Titanic* captain.) Teens often approach risky situations just as the *Titanic* officer approached the iceberg: with a combination of challenge and denial. Teens are aware that such ventures as drinking, drug use, sex, and criminal activity are risky, but they mistakenly believe they can steer around those risks and slide by unharmed. (*I can stop anytime I want,* Kaitlyn told herself.). What they fail to see is the bulk of the danger—addiction, sexually transmitted diseases (STDs), pregnancy, accidents, criminal records, prison, death. Like the *Titanic*, they may have plenty of ballast—courage, responsibility, self-esteem, and other valuable character traits—that will help them stay afloat in a storm, but one mistake in judgment can be deadly. To protect themselves, teens need to recognize their limits and learn to cut their own engines when the situation calls for it.

DRUGS, SEXUALITY, AND VIOLENCE: THE THINK-FEEL-DO CYCLE

While no teen is immune to the temptation of dangerous risks, troubled teens are even more vulnerable. A teen who has low self-esteem or is stressed out is in prime position to get lost in the excitement of drugs, sexuality, or violence and escape the pain and insecurity of self-doubt and anxiety.

Let's consider the Think-Feel-Do Cycle again. Imagine the typical failure cycle of a teenage boy who's shy around girls and lacks the confidence or skills to approach them. He's at a party and is offered a beer. **Read the cycle clockwise, one number at a time.**

EVENT
1. At party; offered beer
5. Drinking with the group

THINK
2. "Sure. Everyone else is drinking."
6. "This is cool. Maybe I'll have another."

FEEL
3. Relieved to be fitting in
7. A little drunk, and less self-conscious around girls

DO
4. He drinks a beer.
8. Laughing and having fun... and having another beer.

We've all heard that alcohol can give a person "courage." What it actually does is create false courage, a shortcut that enables the drinker to get by for a little while without developing real social skills and true courage. But to maintain the illusion, he has to keep getting drunk or high on other drugs. This is where addiction starts. When a teen relies more and more on alcohol or drugs, he loses crucial opportunities to develop social and emotional skills.

The same thing can happen with sex. The pleasure and thrill of sex helps many teenagers temporarily forget their problems. Or teens may turn to sex to boost their confidence, to raise their social standing, to rebel against authority, as a substitute for more difficult ways to get to know one another, or any number of misguided ideas. Once a teen starts using sex as a shortcut like this, it becomes more and more difficult for him to achieve real success.

TEEN DEPRESSION

Depression is a serious condition that affects about one out of every five teens to some extent. The harm it can do is both emotional and physical. Teen depression often grows out of the discouragement of trying to cope with mounting pressures from many different directions—school, home life, social life, sexuality—compounded by the confusion of growing up and moving towards independence. For a depressed teen, feelings of sadness, despair, or anger can become overwhelming and, if left untreated, can infiltrate every aspect of life and lead the teen toward dangerous and harmful behavior like drug use, reckless sexuality, physically harming oneself or others, and even suicide.

The good news is that depression is treatable, and lots of help is available. The first step towards getting help is to know what depression looks and feels like. Often the warning signs of depression are misread as just another teenage phase. But depression is more than a prolonged bout of moodiness or sadness. It's a condition that can have serious repercussions if it goes untreated. Learn to recognize the symptoms of depression in yourself and others.

SYMPTOMS OF DEPRESSION*

- Persistent sadness or hopelessness
- Irritability, anger, or hostility
- Frequent crying
- Apathy (not caring)
- Withdrawal from most friends or family
- Loss of interest in friends or activities
- Negative changes in eating or sleeping habits

- Restlessness and agitation
- Lack of energy
- Feelings of worthlessness or guilt
- Difficulty concentrating
- Unexplained aches and pains
- Extreme sensitivity to criticism
- Mentions of suicide or death

The more symptoms that are present and the longer they've lasted, the more likely the teen is depressed. If you see a number of these signs in yourself or someone you know, don't ignore them. Seek out an adult who you trust to listen, and explain what's going on. An adult can also help you find a counselor or therapist who specializes in adolescent depression.

Unfortunately some depressed teens try to commit suicide. This is the third leading cause of death among 15- to 24-year-olds* and many more suicide attempts are unsuccessful. In addition to the signs of depression, the following warning signs indicate a risk of suicide:

WARNING SIGNS OF SUICIDE RISK*

- Talking or joking about suicide
- Expressions of hopelessness: "I might as well be dead."
- Glorifying death: "I bet people will remember me after I'm gone."
- Saying goodbye to friends and family

- Having accidents or engaging in reckless behavior
- Giving away favorite possessions (preparing for death)
- Seeking out weapons, pills, or other ways to commit suicide

If you find yourself considering suicide, or if you have reason to believe that someone you know is considering it, don't wait; call a suicide hotline or 911.

* This information is from the Centers for Disease Control

In a perfect world, preventing teens from getting knocked off course by drugs, sex, and violence is a team effort with parents, other adults, peers, and the teens themselves all playing a part. But since this is YOUR LIFE we're talking about, the major responsibility is yours. In this chapter and the next, we'll be presenting ten practical, real-world strategies you can use to take control of your life and navigate through your teenage years without hitting any icebergs. These strategies will continue to work for you even after your teen years, and they work well for parents, too. (In fact, if you're in a *Families in Action* group, your parent(s) will be learning these same strategies, but with the goal of helping you, their teen, reduce the risks and prepare for independence.)

To use the Ten Risk-Prevention Strategies for Teens to their full potential, put special effort into two important aspects of your life:

1. Build strong relationships.

Without good relationships, especially with your parents and other family members, it's easier to become discouraged and look for easy, yet harmful, ways to feel better. This book is full of skills you can use to improve your relationships. Remember, you always have a choice about what you say and do.

2. Build your character.

A strong character gives you the ability to face life's challenges head-on, without resorting to drugs and other quick fixes. Fill your ship with the ballast of courage, responsibility, cooperation, mutual respect, and self-esteem, and keep practicing your self-discipline, communication, and problem solving skills.

When you use the ten strategies, you'll draw from the strength of your relationships and character, and in return, the more you use these strategies, the stronger your relationships and character will become! With that in mind, let's start with our first strategy.

10 Risk-Prevention Strategies for TEENS

STRATEGY #1: FIND POSITIVE ROLE MODELS.

If you had to figure out everything in life on your own, you'd better hope you could live a thousand years. Fortunately, a lot of what we need to know can be learned from watching and talking to others. You've probably already learned a few things this way: a skateboard trick or soccer move, a computer skill or video game technique, how to change a tire, repair a bicycle, or any number of other skills. Other people can teach you how to do something by doing it themselves or by *modeling* how to do it, maybe without either of you even knowing that you're learning from them.

Did you know that you also learn a lot of your values and beliefs this way, also without being aware of it? We often watch others to learn how to behave in certain situations, or our *roles*. For example, an older brother may model how to behave when you're romantically interested in someone; a friend may model how to be a student; a parent may model how to be a man or a woman. A *role model* is someone you regard as a good example to follow.

What makes a "good example"? You have to use your judgment to decide. For example, if the skateboarder you're watching tries to jump off the roof and do a 360 flip but wipes out and breaks his legs, you probably aren't going to model your skateboarding on his behavior. However, the real-life experience of choosing a role model is usually not that straightforward. The trouble is that **a role model's behavior and values may be positive, negative, or a combination of both, but no role model is perfect.** So, it pays to learn which aspects of a role model to follow and which to avoid. In other words…

ADOPT THE BEST AND LET GO OF THE REST.

What this means is: Only follow your role models' best examples—their positive traits and behaviors. *Don't* follow their poor examples—their mistakes and negative traits.

For example, you may know someone who's really good about standing up for friends, a quality you'd like to have, too, but he doesn't care much about doing well at school. You can take the best—standing up for friends—and let go of the poor attitude about school.

There aren't rules for how to choose a good role model. It's a personal decision that reflects your unique character and goals. But we *can* give you a few ideas about what to look for. Make this list your own by adding some new ideas and crossing out any you don't like.

A POSITIVE ROLE MODEL IS...

- ☐ Someone who has a good balance between the desire to stay safe and healthy and the desire to take reasonable risks.

- ☐ Someone who has a good balance between work and play and knows that both are important.

- ☐ Someone who follows the rules (and the law) or acts with courage to change them. *Not* someone who sneaks, cheats, or just does what he wants regardless of rules.

- ☐ Someone who shows respect for others, including people who are different from her.

- ☐ Someone who uses effective methods to resolve conflicts, manages anger well, and solves problems without violence.

- ☐ A person of integrity: Someone whose behavior is in line with what she says she values.

- ☐ Someone with values and behavior that you would like to develop in yourself.

- ☐ _____

- ☐ _____

two things about parents as role models

Parents can be great role models. But beware the temptation to expect them to be perfect. Like all role models, parents have a combination of positive and negative qualities, some of which you'll want to follow, others you may not.

#1 None of us can learn everything we need to learn in life from our parents. We have to supplement our knowledge, skills, and values with what we learn from others. You won't get to where you want to be in life without some help along the way from people outside your family unit. This is true no matter how great your parents are or how great anyone else's parents seem to be.

#2 That said, parents are a tremendously important part of life, even if you're upset with them (or they're upset with you) half the time. Parenting is one of the most important and challenging jobs a person can ever have, and because it's so challenging, no one does it perfectly. If you choose someday to become a parent yourself, you'll make mistakes, too. In the meantime, strive to appreciate the gifts your parents have to give you, forgive them when they fall short, and be wise about what lessons you learn from them and what you let go of.

talk to them!

We can learn a lot just by watching our role models, but when it comes to learning values and behavior, sometimes it's more helpful to actually talk to them. Take advantage of any opportunity you get to talk with a role model about values or attitudes, particularly when the subject is something you're curious or uncertain about. The following guidelines can help:

- **SHOW RESPECT.** You're entitled to your own opinions, but make an effort to express them in ways that show respect to the other person. That way, you'll continue to strengthen the relationship even if you disagree. Eye rolls, expletives, and angry outbursts are not respectful ways of disagreeing.

- **LISTEN. REALLY LISTEN.** It's easy to tune out another person who's saying something that you disagree with, don't want to hear, or isn't interesting to you. Parents and other role models may not be as gifted at expressing their beliefs as the actors on TV and movie dramas. They probably won't be able to mesmerize you with a touching story or a rousing Hollywood ending. And they will almost never be accompanied by tear-jerking background music. But they still might have an important message to give you, so don't let these things get in your way of really listening to what your role models say.

- **KEEP AN OPEN MIND.** Again, you don't have to agree with everything a role model says, but you may benefit from keeping an open mind. As you gain more information, you may eventually come to see the wisdom in their values, or they may come to see the wisdom in yours. People who let themselves learn from one another will learn more and have stronger relationships.

Written by Michael H. Popkin. Art by Ron Wheeler.

- **DON'T BE A REVERSE PUPPET.** Most teens want to think for themselves, and they resent being told what values to have and how to behave. They don't want to be puppets who just do and think what they're told. While independent thinking is generally a good thing, some teens lose sight of what they really believe and become *reverse puppets*. With a regular puppet, the puppet master pulls the string for an arm and that arm goes up. But with a reverse puppet, when the puppet master pulls the string for the right arm, the left arm goes up, and vice versa. The reverse puppet believes that he's acting independently, but in truth, he's being controlled by the puppet master just as much as the regular puppet.

For example, Jonathan's parents were often disrespectful and overly demanding of him about his schoolwork, and he resented it. They insisted on better grades but offered little encouragement or support. To show his parents that he wouldn't put up with this treatment, Jonathan stopped doing homework and studying for tests. He started skipping classes and then whole days of school. His grades fell, and eventually he dropped out of school altogether.

It was understandable that Jonathan was unhappy with his parents' harsh treatment, but the way he chose to deal with it was counterproductive. He thought he was rebelling against injustice, but he was really just being a reverse puppet, doing the opposite of what his parents wanted in an effort to "show them!" The irony is that Jonathan really did see the value of doing well in school. By rebelling, he was sacrificing his own beliefs and drastically reducing his chances of success in the future.

Sometimes the hardest thing is to do what you really want to do... when it's also something that an authority figure wants you to do.

You can learn to think for yourself and develop your own philosophy of life without having to become a reverse puppet. Successful, independent-thinking people adopt a lot of their positive values from other people, and they leave behind the values they don't want. That's what it means to "adopt the best and let go of the rest."

How do YOU measure up as a role model?

Just as you pick up some of your values and behaviors from watching adults, peers, and older teens, other people—most likely, younger kids in your family, at school, and in your neighborhood—learn how to act by watching *you*. They look up to you. So, how do you measure up as a role model? Complete the following questionnaire to find out.

As you think about your answers to the questions below, ask yourself whether you're a positive role model, particularly for younger children. If the answer is "YES," good for you! You're probably in a success cycle. If the answer is "NO," you may be in a failure cycle or heading towards one. There's no better time than the present to get back on track. However, if you're too far into a failure cycle to pull yourself out, there are people who can help you: family members, neighbors, teachers, counselors, social workers, doctors, psychologists, and spiritual leaders. Reach out.

1. Describe a time when you behaved responsibly around younger children.

   _____

   _____

2. How do you settle disagreements with other students at school?

   _____

   _____

Continued on next page

3. How old do you think a person should be to drink alcoholic beverages? To smoke cigarettes?

    _____

    _____

4. Describe a time when you were able to stand up to negative peer pressure and tell someone "no" when he or she asked you to do something that you knew was illegal, against school rules, or against your family's values or rules of conduct?

    _____

    _____

5. Have you ever asked a brother, a sister, or a friend to lie for you because you knew what you were doing wasn't the right thing to do? If so, describe that situation.

    _____

    _____

6. Name some older teens at your school whom you respect. What do you respect about them?

    _____

    _____

7. Describe a time when you had trouble controlling how you acted because you got really angry.

    _____

    _____

8. Imagine yourself in 25 years with a 13-year-old son or daughter. Would you be happy if your son or daughter had a person like you are today as a best friend? Why or why not?

    _____

    _____

9. When do you think you'll be ready to become sexually involved with another person?

    _____

    _____

how did we get on the topic of sex?

You may have been surprised to see that last item on the questionnaire: *When do you think you'll be ready to become sexually involved with another person?* If we're going to talk about the positive values teens can learn from good role models, we've got to talk a little bit about sexuality.

There are two important goals for teens to achieve with regard to their sexuality:

GOAL #1: To accept that you're a sexual being

Sex is a natural part of life, and sexuality is a natural part of being human. Having sexual feelings is a normal part of adolescence and certainly nothing to be ashamed of. But what you do with those feelings, like most things, can be for better or for worse.

GOAL #2: To develop a value system and philosophy of life as a foundation from which you can make decisions about sexuality

Before you start making decisions about sex, you need to form an idea of who you are and what you want in life. Without this foundation of values, you'll be more likely to let sexual pressures and other outside forces make choices for you. Try on some of the following values about sexuality and see how they fit.

VALUES ABOUT SEXUALITY

- Sexuality is a natural and healthy part of life.
- Sex can be meaningful when it's an expression of love.
- Always treat yourself and others with respect.
- It's foolish to have unprotected sex (unless you're married).
- Or…It's foolish to have sex outside of marriage at all.
- You are responsible for any child you help create. Be aware of that before you have sex.
- Pornography and other forms of lust-driven sex can distort one's idea of sexuality and may become addictive.

You may not agree with all the values listed here. That's OK. The idea is to clarify your own values and think about what role models you will choose to learn from.

STRATEGY #2: EDUCATE YOURSELF ABOUT THE RISKS OF DRUGS, SEXUALITY, AND VIOLENCE.

Teens get a lot of information about drugs, sexuality, and violence from other teens. Unfortunately, much of this information is either inaccurate or incomplete because teens often give one-sided accounts, emphasizing the exciting aspects while downplaying or ignoring the risks. So just because you've talked about these topics with your friends, don't assume that you know the facts. You need some additional sources. There are plenty of those to choose from: books, web sites, movies, TV, school, your parents, and other adults, and lots more.

finding reliable info

But how can you trust that the information you're getting is accurate?

Consider the source.

Is the information coming from a well-informed person or an established organization with a reputation for giving accurate information? Avoid sources that are known to give misinformation or report rumors. Also avoid sources that mix opinions in with facts. They might be misleading you to serve their own purposes.

Use more than one source.

The more trusted sources you have giving you the same information, the more likely it's true.

Check your own gut feelings.

Does the information feel right to you, or does something smell funny about it? When in doubt, look for more information or other sources.

School is one place teens can get good information about drugs, sexuality, and violence, and we're not talking about the information you pick up through the grapevine of schoolmates. Many schools have programs to inform teens and draw their attention to the real dangers of substance use, sexual behavior, and violence. But schools are usually limited when it comes to discussing the values associated with these topics. For that, your best bet may be (take a deep breath, and don't panic)…

Yes, seriously. Your parents won't know everything there is to know about these subjects, but they have the benefit of experience. They may have even made some mistakes that you can learn from. And when they don't have an answer, you can research the question together.

If you want to find out more about drugs, sexuality, and violence from your parents but you're not sure where to start, try one of the topics in the "So, what will you talk about?" box below.

so, what will you talk about?

Here are a few of the many topics around the subject of drugs, sexuality, and violence you could discuss with your parents.

TOBACCO, ALCOHOL, AND OTHER DRUGS

- Specific drugs, their effects and risks (including nicotine, alcohol, and marijuana)

- The physical, psychological, and social effects of using any drug

- The consequences of breaking the law

- The increased chances of engaging in other risky behavior while under the influence of a drug (for example, having unprotected sex while under the influence of alcohol.)

SEXUALITY

- The reproductive process and birth control; whether you believe in abstinence, natural family planning, or methods such as condoms or pills; the risks and benefits of each.

- Sexually transmitted diseases (STDs): AIDS (still a big risk!), herpes, syphilis, gonorrhea, chlamydia, HPV, and others.

VIOLENCE

- Stranger danger: What situations leave a teen vulnerable to rape, abduction, or other violence by a stranger; how to reduce these risks

- Fighting: How conflicts grow into fights; the risks of fighting; what you could do instead; what to do if you're on the sidelines of a fight

- Date violence: How common it is; why physical force is wrong; what to do if it happens to you or someone you know

- Relationship abuse: What behavior should be considered abusive; how to identify an abusive relationship; what to do if you or someone you know is in an abusive relationship

The following dialogue can help you get an idea of how a discussion with a parent might go. It's an example of a parent-teen talk about AIDS and other sexually transmitted diseases. You may want to show this to your parent. Using it as a discussion starter could help to break the ice.

Father: You've probably heard a lot about sexually transmitted diseases (STDs). I thought we should talk about it ourselves. First of all, what do you know about them?

Son: Why do you think I need to know about that?

Father: Well, there are a lot of things teenagers need to know about. This is just one of them.

Son: Oh, well, I know they are called STDs because you can get them from having sex. I know that syphilis and gonorrhea are two of them...oh, yeah and AIDS.

Father: Right, and Herpes, Chlamydia, HPV, and lots of other stuff.

Son: Wow, that's a lot of nasty stuff.

Father: You are right about that.

Son: But they can cure them all, right?

Father: Well, they can cure most of them, if they catch it in time. But not all of them. How much do you know about AIDS?

Son: AIDS is a disease that can kill you. That it has to do with the immune system. And that you can get it from having sex with a gay guy.

Father: Well, that's partially right. It is a disease that affects the body's immune system. In fact, the word AIDS actually stands for Acquired Immune Deficiency Syndrome. In other words, it attacks the body's immune system, leaving the person helpless to fight off diseases. People who get AIDS eventually die from some other disease, because their bodies can't fight it off anymore.

Son: Yeah, I remember now, it sort of takes away their defenses.

Father: Exactly. And you're also right about it being sexually transmitted. Because the AIDS virus is carried in blood and in semen, most people who get AIDS get it from sexual intercourse. But some people have also gotten AIDS from blood transfusions, although this is more rare because people are testing blood better than they used to. Also, some drug users get it from sharing needles.

Son: Yeah, I saw that on a movie one time. This guy got AIDS from shooting up with a needle that a guy with AIDS had used.

Father: Right, the needle was infected. But there is one thing that you're a little bit off on.

Son: What's that?

Father: People don't get AIDS only from gays. In fact, the AIDS virus doesn't know a gay person from a straight person from a bisexual person. All it knows is it can be transmitted through blood and semen, which means that it can also be carried through regular heterosexual intercourse.

Son: Well, at least they can cure it now.

Father: Not so fast. They have made a lot of progress in treating AIDS, and there are treatments now that let people live a lot longer with it than they used to. But there is still no cure.

Son: Well, how can you keep from getting it? Is there a vaccine?

Father: No, not yet. The only sure way to keep from getting AIDS is not to have sex.

Son: I'm supposed to never have sex?!

Father: Well it doesn't have to be quite that drastic. If you wait until you get married, and you're sure that your partner doesn't have AIDS, and if the two of you are faithful during your marriage, then you can be 100% sure that you can be as sexual as you want to be and not get AIDS.

Son: Can't you use a condom or something like that?

Father: Probably. If you use them correctly, they're supposed to prevent AIDS in most cases. But they're not 100% safe.

Son: Well, if I ever had sex before getting married, I think I'd use one.

Father: Well, I hope you decide to wait until you're married. But if you don't, I'm real glad to hear you say that. In fact, I'd say that anybody who has sex these days without a condom is risking their lives. I came across a web site that I think you'll find interesting. It's got some good information about AIDS and other sexually transmitted diseases. I'll e-mail you the link, and then I'd like to hear your opinion about it.

THE CASE FOR WAITING

If you're participating in the *Families in Action* program with your parents, you'll be doing the following activity in your group, but you can also do it on your own.

Teens hear a lot about the importance of waiting to have a sexual relationship until they're more mature or married. Have you ever really thought about *why* this is important? In the blanks below, list ten reasons why it makes sense to wait until you're an adult or even married to become sexually intimate with another person. You don't necessarily have to believe your own arguments; just pretend that this is a debate and you have to argue the "It's worth waiting for" side.

1. _____

2. _____

3. _____

4. _____

5. _____

6. _____

7. _____

8. _____

9. _____

10. _____

10 Risk-Prevention Strategies for TEENS

STRATEGY #3: FILTER <u>OUT</u> NEGATIVE INFLUENCES AND <u>IN</u> POSITIVE ONES.

Teens who have positive people in their lives are much more likely to get into a success cycle than teens on their own, and they're less likely to get involved with drugs, irresponsible sexuality, or violence. But positive influences aren't the only influences out there. There are also negative influences: people and events in your life that can actually push you towards engaging in risky behavior.

garbage in, garbage out (GIGO)

"Garbage in, garbage out" is a saying in the fields of computer science and information technology. It's used to point out that a computer will unquestioningly process the most nonsensical input data (garbage in) and from it produce nonsensical output (garbage out). The quality of output is determined by the quality of the input. If we applied this idea to our Think-Feel-Do Cycle, it would look something like this…

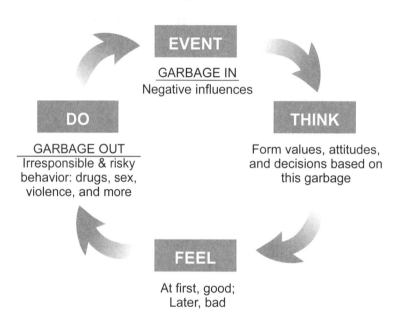

GARBAGE IN, GARBAGE OUT

EVENT
GARBAGE IN
Negative influences

THINK
Form values, attitudes, and decisions based on this garbage

FEEL
At first, good; Later, bad

DO
GARBAGE OUT
Irresponsible & risky behavior: drugs, sex, violence, and more

Negative influences might feel good at first, but later they feel bad because they have undesirable consequences. When we put garbage into our system, at first we see it as the truth, as something good for us. Taking drugs for the first time might feel like a positive, fun thing to do, but later, when the negative consequences start showing up, it's revealed to be a negative influence after all. Some of the negative influences that put garbage into our system are:

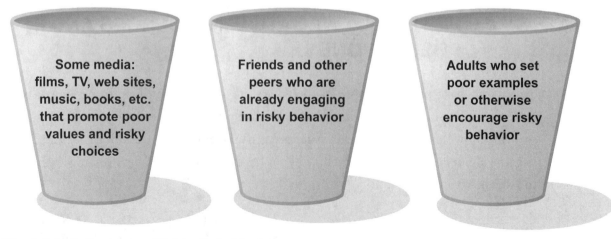

Some media: films, TV, web sites, music, books, etc. that promote poor values and risky choices

Friends and other peers who are already engaging in risky behavior

Adults who set poor examples or otherwise encourage risky behavior

filtering OUT negative influences

Although there will always be times when you're exposed to negative influences, there are lots of ways to limit the amount of garbage that gets into your system. For example:

- Limit the media you use to those that present positive messages.

- Negotiate with your parents to set reasonable curfews for both weeknights and weekend nights, and abide by them.

- Make sure your parents always know where you are and check in periodically.

- Politely avoid spending too much time with people who are on a path you don't want to be on.

- Be especially careful of where you go on the Internet. Not only to keep out garbage, but also actual predators (More about this in the "Going Online" section on pages 168-169) .

- Don't believe everything you read, hear, or see. There is a lot of misinformation out there.

filtering IN positive events

If you can filter *out* certain events that might harm or negatively influence you, you can also filter *in* positive events that can help build character and lead to a success cycle. Look for opportunities to n learn from positive adult role models and other positive teens. For example:

- Youth groups
- Organized sports
- School clubs and groups
- Relatives
- Mentoring programs such as Big Brothers/Big Sisters
- Positive media
- Summer camp and other away-from-home programs
- Spiritual education opportunities

GOING ONLINE

You may have trouble imagining how anyone did anything before the Internet, cell phones, and other modern communication devices. . The way young people communicate, socialize, and meet new people are pretty different from what your parents and grandparents knew when they were teens, when they had to either pick up the phone or meet a friend in person to have a conversation. Now when we want to communicate, we can do it through e-mail, texting, blogging, chat rooms, forums, media swapping, social networking sites, and the list goes on.

New media has revolutionized the way we communicate, learn, do business, and have fun, but it has also brought new risks: risks to your physical safety, your privacy, your reputation, your emotional well-being, and even your future college and work prospects. So it's vital that you know what the risks are and how you can avoid them.

SOCIAL NETWORKING SITES: AVOIDING THE RISKS

Using social networking sites is often just harmless fun, a way for teens and everyone else to keep in touch with one another and share what matters to them (as well as what doesn't matter much, like what they ate for breakfast, what they're watching on TV, and many other fascinating pieces of information). But sometimes the things that teens post about themselves or others can do harm in real life. Follow these basic guidelines to avoid the risks.

Protect access to your information. If you're going to put information about yourself online, take precautions to keep from accidentally making it available to the wrong people. Use the security settings on the social networking site so that only people you know and trust will be able to see your information. Use a strong password to reduce the chance of someone accessing your account. If someone does hack into your account, report it to the site and to your parents immediately, and change all of your other account passwords to prevent further damage.

Watch what you post.   Never post anything about yourself that shows or describes you drinking alcohol, taking drugs, engaging in sexual behavior, or anything else that you wouldn't want your parents, your school principal, or your boss at work to see. Once it's on the Internet, this information may be available for years and years, and it may come back to haunt you when you apply for college or interview for a job. Likewise, be careful with what you post about other people. The words you type and the photos or videos you post may have the power to seriously hurt other people.

Stand up to cyberbullies. If you get into a situation where someone is spreading rumors or otherwise defaming your character on a social networking site, or if this is happening to someone you know, there are actions you can take. Tell your parents or other trusted adults. Cooperate with them to contact the social networking site to make a complaint or go directly to the person responsible, if you know who that is. Depending on how serious the act is, you may even be justified in calling the police.

Be wary. The Internet is a perfect place for people who wish to disguise their identity. Internet predators do exist, and teenagers are their primary target. Be suspicious of anyone who wants to know too much about you or seems to be trying too hard to help you. Never agree to meet an online acquaintance by yourself or in an isolated location. If you want to meet a longtime Internet friend in person, tell your parents about it. Arrange a meeting where you'll be around other people, and don't agree to go off alone with the person at any point. This may seem like a paranoid attitude to take, but the danger is very real.

The Internet is also host to predators of a different sort: the sort that wants your money. They're involved in credit card fraud, identity theft, e-mail scams, and countless other ways of stealing money and credit. Never give out a credit card number, bank account number, or social security number unless you're absolutely sure it's a trusted business with a secure site to conduct transactions. Never respond to e-mails or click on advertisements that claim you're entitled to money. If an offer sounds too good to be true, it probably is!

TEXTING AND SEXTING

Text messaging has all but replaced phone conversations for many young people, and it may not be long before something else replaces that. But whatever type of communication you use, keep in mind two important words: **safety** and **respect**. Texting while driving is just plain dangerous. When your eyes are looking down at a phone you can't see what's happening in front of you. Take your eyes off the road for even a second and you could be dead or kill someone else.

And then there's *sexting*: sending sexually explicit messages or pictures of yourself to someone else or encouraging someone else to send them to you. Sexting is both dangerous and disrespectful. It's dangerous because once a photo or message is out there, you never know where it will end up and who will see it. It's disrespectful because it cheapens sexuality and makes it about lust, not love.

10 Risk-Prevention Strategies for TEENS

STRATEGY #4. ESTABLISH CLEAR GUIDELINES FOR BEHAVIOR.

Sometimes teens need help to know when to "cut their engines" (to return to our *Titanic* analogy). Parents can provide that help by working with them to establish guidelines of behavior for difficult or risky situations. Wise parents will negotiate these guidelines with their teens rather than demand compliance. Wise teens will negotiate in good faith, accepting that their parents, as leaders of the family, have the final say.

Working with your parents to set guidelines of behavior for yourself may seem like the last thing an independence-minded teen would want to do, but it's actually a smart move. Chances are, parents are going to impose rules one way or another because they want their teens to stay safe and be successful in life. Wouldn't you rather help decide what those rules will be? Plus, negotiating guidelines and then following them are opportunities for you to demonstrate responsibility and earn more freedom. And most importantly, having established guidelines can really pay off when you're facing a tough decision or a potentially risky situation.

Not every situation in a teen's life calls for guidelines. Most of the time, you'll still have to rely on your own good judgment and strong character to make the right decision when temptation or conflict shows up. Other situations—ones that might involve drugs, sexuality, or violence—are often too risky to allow teens full freedom to make an unwise decision. This is where setting guidelines is not only useful but also smart. For example:

IT'S A GOOD IDEA TO SET GUIDELINES ABOUT:	EXAMPLES OF GUIDELINES
Using alcohol, tobacco, and other drugs	A "no-use" rule*: No use of illegal drugs by anyone in the family, and no use of alcohol or nicotine under the legal age of _____.
Curfews	Be home by 9 PM on weekdays, 11:30 PM on weekends.
Having friends over, or spending nights out	A parent or guardian (an adult) must be present at sleepovers.
Going to parties	No parties where there is no adult supervision or where anyone is using alcohol or other drugs. If you find that they are, call your parents and they'll pick you up.
When and how to use physical force	Never start a fight, but defend yourself if you're attacked. Agree to take a self-defense class.
Going places that could be dangerous	Never go alone. Take two or more friends and a cell phone. Tell your parents where you're going and call them to check in when you arrive.
Dating	Parents must meet any person you're going out with. No interrogations, just a quick meeting.
Driving, or riding with friends	If you suspect that the driver is going to drink or has been drinking, or even if you're not sure, don't agree to ride with him or her.
The use of media	Spend up to an hour per weekday and two hours per weekend day on the Internet or playing video games. Time needed for homework or other school-related research does not count toward the limit.

A Problem-Prevention Talk is a good model to use when you and your parents want to establish guidelines. Remember the five steps:

HAVING A PROBLEM-PREVENTION TALK

1. Identify potential problems and risks.

2. Share thoughts and feelings about these problems and acknowledge others' thoughts and feelings.

3. Generate guidelines through brainstorming and negotiation.

4. Decide on logical consequences for violating guidelines (if necessary).

5. Follow up later to make sure guidelines were followed and to enforce consequences (if necessary).

FAMILY ENRICHMENT ACTIVITY: EXPRESSING LOVE

Building a positive relationship with your parents is an ongoing process, and it takes steady effort. It includes having fun together, learning specific skills, showing respect, and most of all, love. Kids do better when they know that their parents love them. But did you know that parents do better, too, when they know that their kids love them? You can show your parents you love them in lots of little ways: a kiss, a hug, a pat on the back, or just a smile. You can also demonstrate love through your actions: doing what your parents ask, doing things for them *without* being asked, or just spending time with them. But you also need to *tell* your parents that you love them. The words may feel awkward if you're not used to saying them, but they're beautiful to the people who love you, even if they don't know how to respond.

Explore some ways to express love to your parent(s) and other important adults in your life, including actually saying "I love you." The following exercise will help you.

EXPRESSING LOVE

Remember when...

Think about a time when an adult in your life expressed love to you. Maybe it was a parent, a grandparent, another relative, or a teacher. Maybe the expression was through words, maybe through an action like a pat on the back or a hug.

Describe the experience: _____

_____

_____

How did you feel? _____

_____

_____

EXPRESSING LOVE AT HOME

Remember to tell your parent(s) or other important adults in your life that you love them. Write about each experience in the chart below. One example is included.

WHO?	WHAT YOU SAID	HOW THE OTHER PERSON RESPONDED
Mom	"I know I hardly ever say this, but I love you."	"That means a lot to me. I love you, too, honey."
_____	_____	_____
_____	_____	_____
_____	_____	_____
_____	_____	_____

HOME ACTIVITIES

1. Read Chapter 6 in this guide.

2. Complete the "How do you measure up as a role model?" questionnaire on pages 158-159.

2. Have a talk with your parents about sexuality. Use the parent-teen dialog about STDs on page 163 to get started.

3. Find at least one time this week to express love to your parent(s) or another important adult in your life, and complete the guide sheet on page 173.

4. Answer the "Teen Action Report" questions on pages 175.

TEEN ACTION REPORT

Write your responses to the following questions on a separate sheet of paper or in a journal.

about yourself

1. Who are your role models? What qualities of theirs do you wish to emulate?

2. What "garbage" do you need to filter out of your life? What positive influences could you filter in to take its place?

3. Who in your life would you trust to talk honestly with you and provide accurate information about sexuality? What questions would you like them to answer, or what specific issues would you want to discuss?

about your family

1. Who in your family do you consider a role model? What qualities of theirs do you wish to emulate?

2. Who are your other family members' role models? Do you agree with their choices? Why or why not?

3. What are some of your family rules or guidelines? What are some of the consequences for violating them? Do these guidelines and consequences work well? Use the chart below to identify some new guidelines and consequences that you think would make your family life run more smoothly.

GUIDELINE	CONSEQUENCE FOR VIOLATING

about your school

1. In what ways are your friends at school positive role models? How about your teachers, coaches, and other school faculty?

2. What rules or guidelines at your school are particularly important for you to keep in mind?

CHAPTER 6

DRUGS, SEXUALITY, AND VIOLENCE:

Reducing the Risks, Part 2

A young man

A young man stares at his computer screen while his wife and baby sleep. He knows he must stop, that it just isn't worth the risk to his marriage, his family, his job. Yet his fingers at the keyboard seem to automatically take him back to his favorite cyber space haunts whenever he can—sometimes all night. He tells himself this is the last time, but he knows it isn't. His addiction to pornography is too powerful.

A young woman

A young woman pours yet another glass of wine. She knows she drinks too much. And when she drinks she also smokes, another problem. Her doctor has warned her of the consequences, but they seem so far away, nothing that affects her. As her father used to say, *"It's my life, and if a little wine (OK, a lot of wine, she admits) helps me get through the day, so be it."* Feeling a pang of sadness at this memory, she tips her glass and drains it. Her father had died of "alcohol-related causes" in his fifties, which she knows she should take as a clear warning to stop. But not tonight. Tonight she's sad, so she needs it. Tomorrow she'll find some other reason not to stop.

Unless you've experienced the powerlessness of addiction yourself, you may be thinking that the young adults in these stories simply lack the will to give up their bad habits. Many of us don't really understand how a person could be helpless to stop a behavior. We believe that we'd never fall into that trap, that we'd be strong enough to quit before it caused any harm.

That kind of thinking is dangerous, because **none of us are immune to addiction**. If you've experienced addiction in your own life or in a parent or friend, you may have already learned this, and also that there's a big difference between a bad habit and an addiction. Here is some of what we know about addiction:

A FEW THINGS WE KNOW ABOUT ADDICTION

> **ad•dic•tion**   *noun*   \uh-ˈdik-shun\
>
> **:** the state of being enslaved to a habit-forming practice or substance to such an extent that its withdrawal causes severe trauma.

ADDICTION... Addiction can occur whether the chemicals that fuel the addiction are introduced from the outside (as with tobacco, alcohol, and other drugs) or produced inside the brain itself (as with sex, gambling, work, and perhaps even forms of anger and violence).

ADDICTION... Some addictions are stronger than others. For example, a coffee (or caffeine) addiction is mild compared to an addiction to crystal meth (methamphetamine).

ADDICTION... Addiction to one thing doesn't mean that a person has a general tendency to develop addictions. For example, a person who could easily become addicted to pornography is not necessarily at risk for becoming addicted to alcohol.

ADDICTION... Addictive tendencies are genetically passed down through families. A teen whose mother is an alcoholic is eight times more likely to become addicted to alcohol himself.

ADDICTION... The length of time it takes to become fully addicted varies from substance to substance and from person to person. It may take three years for a drinker to develop full-blown alcoholism, while some people become addicted to crack cocaine after a single use.

ADDICTION... Addictive behavior like drinking alcohol, smoking cigarettes, gambling, and viewing pornography often begins as a way to relieve stress and alter one's mood. Many addicts say that their addiction began in adolescence for just this reason.

Another thing we know about addiction is that it usually follows a simple pattern:

Stage 1. **Pleasure**

Stage 2. **Pleasure + problems**

Stage 3. **Problems**

During stage 1, nobody wants to quit. The behavior feels good and you don't see any harmful effects.

During stage 2, you're still getting pleasure out of the behavior, but it's also creating some problems. Maybe your grades start dropping; you get into fights, you argue with your parents and your friends, you don't have money for things you need… There are lots of possibilities. But you crave the pleasure of the addiction, and while you're doing it you still feel good.

During stage 3, however, the addiction stops bringing you pleasure, because you've built up a *tolerance* to the behavior. That means that it takes more and more of the behavior to satisfy your craving for it. You get to a point at which you no longer get real pleasure from the substance; the best that you can do is relieve your withdrawal symptoms so you don't feel sick. From there it's just problems and more problems caused by the addiction. This is when people finally come to treatment, but for many it's too late, and for others it's a long, hard road to recovery that changes their lives forever.

Scientists have made a lot of progress towards understanding addiction. Maybe one day there will be a cure for it. But for now, your best bet is to understand the risks and make smart choices that will keep you from having to cope with addiction down the road.

ADDICTION AND THE TREE OF LIFE

If you are participating in a *Teens in Action* or *Families in Action* program, you'll be doing the following activity in your group, but you can also do it on your own.

What might addiction look like if you let it into your life? Below is an illustration of what we call the Tree of Life. Once the leaves and branches are filled in, this tree represents what a person hopes to achieve in life. The branches are major aspects of life, and the leaves are hopes and goals for each aspect. For example, on your Education branch you might have a "Graduate high school" leaf and a "Get into college" leaf.

Make this Tree of Life your own by writing your hopes and goals on the leaves of the Family, Education, and Career branches. Think of another important area of your life and write it on the blank branch. Then fill in those leaves as well. Go ahead; create a great life for yourself!

Here's a Tree of Life for Jessica, a fifteen-year-old with a pretty normal life and a lot of hopes and dreams for her future.

Except…what's that in the corner? It looks like a swarm of locusts, but what it represents here is an addiction. Jessica hasn't given much thought to addiction. That only happens to other people, she thinks. So when she starts an addictive behavior, she doesn't pay much attention to it. She's enjoying its pleasures, and she hasn't seen any negative effects yet, so no worries, right?

Now the swarm is close enough to the Tree that a few locusts are moving in and starting to eat the leaves. What's happening in Jessica's life now? She's started to have some problems. Her grades drop a little. Some friends notice she's acting differently. She gets reprimanded at her job. But she's still experiencing some pleasure from her addictive behavior, so she keeps on doing it and finds some way to justify it to herself. She ignores the holes growing larger and larger on her leaves, until…

Now Jessica's got serious problems. She's failing classes. She argues with her parents every time they try to talk. She doesn't feel comfortable with any of her old friends anymore. And she could be fired from her job any day now. Her present life is so full of problems that it takes all her energy just to get by day to day. She doesn't think much about her future anymore. As she lets things slide—her grades, her relationships, her self-esteem—those hopes and dreams she had for her future are moving beyond her reach. We can see where this is heading if Jessica doesn't get treatment for her addiction…

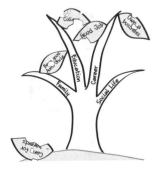

This is the life that addiction left for Jessica. Addiction may not kill you. It may not take *everything* that you have. But it sure is capable of doing both, especially without treatment.

some ways to avoid addiction

It's obviously better not to become addicted in the first place rather than hope you'll recover from it if you do. But how do you avoid addiction when pretty much anything that gives you pleasure can become addictive? Here are a few ways to protect yourself from addiction.

1. **Avoid things that are known to be highly addictive.**

   Some things are more addictive than others, so especially avoid drugs like heroin and other opiates (like pain pills), crystal meth and other narcotics, tobacco (one of the hardest addictions to break), and anything else you know is highly addictive.

2. **If you choose to drink, wait until you're an adult.**

   There are a number of good reasons for this, but I'll focus on two now. The research shows that the longer you wait to start drinking, the less likely you are to get addicted and let your brain development be affected.

3. **Avoid binging on anything.**

   Binging –which means doing way too much of a substance or behavior– is not only dangerous in its own right, but it also accelerates the addiction process.

4. **Spread out even healthy pleasure over a number of activities.**

   Find a number of ways to bring pleasure into your life. If the only thing you enjoy doing is playing video games, that can become addictive. So can food, sports, and even work. By broadening the field of what gives you pleasure, you can keep your brain from craving any one thing.

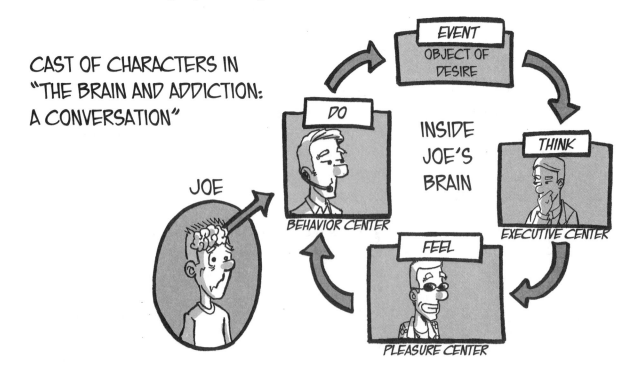

CAST OF CHARACTERS IN "THE BRAIN AND ADDICTION: A CONVERSATION"

JOE

INSIDE JOE'S BRAIN

EVENT — OBJECT OF DESIRE

DO — BEHAVIOR CENTER

THINK — EXECUTIVE CENTER

FEEL — PLEASURE CENTER

Written by Michael H. Popkin. Art by Joseba Morales.

THE END

Addiction isn't the only risk you take when you get involved with drugs, sexuality, or violence. It also puts your health, safety, good judgment, success, and your very life at risk. Our Ten Risk-Prevention Strategies for Teens, which we started in Chapter 5, are a set of tools that can help you avoid such outcomes. So let's get back to them. So far we've covered four of the ten strategies:

1. **Find positive role models.**
2. **Educate yourself about the risks.**
3. **Filter <u>out</u> negative influences and <u>in</u> positive ones.**
4. **Establish clear guidelines for behavior.**

In this chapter we'll present the remaining six strategies:

5. **Make sure there's adult supervision.**
6. **Work with other teens and adults.**
7. **Find healthy opportunities for challenge.**
8. **Learn to resist peer pressure.**
9. **Identify and confront high-risk behavior.**
10. **Calmly manage a crisis.**

10 Risk-Prevention Strategies for **TEENS**

STRATEGY #5: MAKE SURE THERE'S ADULT SUPERVISION.

Not too long ago, the news reported a story about a fight that broke out between teens from rival high schools at a party. There'd been a lot of drinking, and passions—as well as tensions—were high. During the fight, one teen pulled a knife and stabbed another, who died on the way to the hospital. This took place in an affluent suburb of a typical American city.

You may expect that the parents of the house were out of town, as is often the case with teen parties. They weren't. In fact, they were upstairs watching TV. When asked why they weren't downstairs supervising the party, they answered, *"Because we didn't want to get in the way."*

Their response isn't that unusual. A lot of teens might think it would be great for their parents (and friends' parents) to just leave them alone to do whatever they want. But it's part of a parent's job to get in the way, and there are reasons for that. Remember the teen brain research we first introduced in Chapter 1? Teens' brains are in the process of developing the ability to make judgments about complicated issues and set reasonable limits for themselves, but they're not quite there yet. Until they get there, parents and other adults have the responsibility of providing safe limits on their teens' freedom. This means that in any situation that might involve risk to teens, responsible adults need to supervise. Teens who accept these limits gracefully are putting themselves on a more successful path. Along the way, they will earn more freedom through good choices and responsible behavior.

Make sure your parents or other in-charge adult knows where you are and who you're with. A lot of teens resist this idea, but it accomplishes two very important goals. First, it helps keep you safe. Look what happened to the guy in the movie *127 hours* (a true story). The main character, a young man with a passion for boulder climbing and a serious independent streak, didn't tell anyone he was going alone to a remote climbing spot in the desert. He had an accident that got his arm caught between two rocks. Days later, when nobody had come to rescue him (because nobody knew where he was), he had to cut off his own arm with a pocket knife to save his life.

So, if you don't want to cut your own arm off with a pocketknife, make sure an adult always knows where you're going. Besides keeping you safe, this will also help build trust between you and your parents. When you're where you say you'll be, you check in when you say you will, and you generally stay on your parents' radar, you're actually training them to trust you. This trust should pay out in the form of greater freedom.

Negotiate and abide by curfews. Some teens think of a curfew as a cruel restriction of their freedom, but a curfew may be more accurately described as a stepping stone on the path between living under your parents' protection and real independence. Abiding by a curfew helps structure your time and, by setting some limits to your night's activities, keeps you safer. As a result, the folks at home worry less about your safety while you're out. You and your parents can negotiate reasonable curfews for school nights and weekends. Your parents have the final say in this negotiation, but the more responsible your behavior has been, the stronger your negotiating power!

STRATEGY #6: **WORK WITH OTHER TEENS AND PARENTS**

There's a saying about "strength in numbers." If you want to make your family, school, community, or even your planet a better place, your best bet is to work with others to bring about change. Teens in action with other teens and adults can be a powerful force, regardless of whether it's applied towards a constructive or *de*structive goal. On the destructive side, gangs often use their power to intimidate and hurt others both inside and outside their group. On the positive side, a group of teens standing together to resist bullies, gangs, drugs, and other harmful influences has a much better chance of success than a single teen standing alone. Teens working with others have made huge strides towards justice, equality, and prosperity around the world.

STRATEGY #7: **FIND HEALTHY OPPORTUNITIES FOR CHALLENGE.**

When I was seventeen, I had the opportunity to experience a month-long "Outward Bound" course in the Blue Ridge Mountains. Every morning at daybreak, we were roused from our sleep to run three miles to a mountain stream where we were doused in ice-cold water. The day only got harder after that: We ran, hiked, climbed, and otherwise pitted ourselves against the elements. It was the most physically demanding experience of my life, but when it was over, I felt that I had really achieved something.

- Dr. Michael Popkin

We humans love a good challenge. This is especially true when we're teenage humans. Whether it's riding a thrill ride at a theme park, learning a new bike trick, or solving a difficult math proof, the excitement of meeting a challenge releases chemicals in our bodies that make us feel good, and motivate us to keep achieving. Unfortunately, like most goals, the goal of challenging oneself can be approached through *positive adventures* or more dangerous *thrill-seeking* behavior.

Many teens have a hard time finding enough positive adventures to satisfy them, so they resort to *thrill seeking* just to feel a rush of adrenaline and a sense of adventure. Drugs, sex, and violence offer easy but dangerous ways to accomplish this goal.

You can find lots of positive ways to challenge yourself if you look for them, and that means being open to new experiences that might kindle a hidden passion. Finding things you're interested in learning about or doing not only helps you challenge yourself, it also makes you a more interesting person.

If it's a physical challenge you want, look into adrenaline-pumping activities like…

ORGANIZED SPORTS:
school teams
community leagues
youth groups (Boys and Girls Clubs, YMCA)

MOUNTAIN BIKING

hiking

SKATING

white-water rafting

rock climbing
(But not alone!)

OUTWARD BOUND
OR OTHER OUTDOOR
ADVENTURE PROGRAMS

scouting

If you like challenges of a more intellectual or artistic nature and get satisfaction from developing your skills and knowledge, try something like…

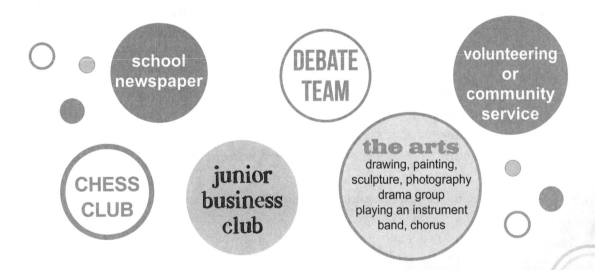

school newspaper

DEBATE TEAM

volunteering or community service

CHESS CLUB

junior business club

the arts
drawing, painting, sculpture, photography
drama group
playing an instrument
band, chorus

These are just a few of the possibilities. If you can find an interest that challenges you to stick with it and do your best, you'll do more than satisfy your need for excitement; you'll also kick your Spiral of Success (belonging, learning, and contributing) into high gear and reach new levels of courage and self-esteem.

STRATEGY #8: LEARN TO RESIST PEER PRESSURE.

Most people realize that to "just say no" to drugs, sex, or violence is a lot easier said than done. Humans have a very strong need to belong. From prehistoric times, our very survival has depended on belonging to various groups, from clans to communities to civilizations. As teens move from their "home group" of family towards independence, the desire to find other groups to belong to becomes very strong.

Have you ever found yourself doing something you didn't really want to do because your friends, or people you wanted as friends, were doing it? Have you laughed at something because your friends thought it was funny? Have you worn trendy jeans or sneakers because "everyone's wearing them"? Or how about this: Have you participated in a standing ovation at the end of a performance just because most of the audience was doing it? We all have! This subtle pressure to go along (or "conform") with a group is often called *peer pressure*, but in reality what we see more is *peer conformity*. It's actually pretty rare for teens to actively "pressure" other teens to do drugs or other high-risk activities. More often, what happens is a friend or acquaintance offers you the opportunity do something, and you do it, thinking you're freely choosing to participate. But usually what you're really choosing is to conform to the group. Since people often prefer to be friends with others who share their interests, the unconscious thinking is that in order for people to like you, you should do the things they like to do. Take smoking, for example. If the group likes to smoke, you may think you have a better chance of being "in" with the group if you smoke too. No one is pressuring you outwardly, but the pressure is there just the same.

This desire to fit in makes it tough to be a free-thinking young person. But if you go through life doing whatever it takes to be accepted by others, you'll lose opportunities to develop your own unique self. And you'll probably cause yourself a lot of stress, trying to conform to other people's ideas that aren't right fper you. Thinking for yourself and making your own choices takes courage, sometimes a lot of it, but it pays off well. In return you get self-esteem, self-respect, and more courage.

So, whether you're actually pressured to do something you don't believe in or just feel the internal desire to conform and fit in, you need the ability to resist in a way that feels good to you. For this you need three main things:

1. **Knowing your rights**
2. **The courage to do what's right**
3. **A good comeback line**

Let's go over these one by one.

1. Knowing your rights

This means recognizing that you have the right to say "no" to peer pressure. Your goals and the values you want for your life are important. You also have the right to determine what's cool for you. Sometimes this may mean going along with the group, and other times it may mean choosing a different path.

2. The courage to do what's right

We all have an obligation to do the right thing as best we can determine, and sometimes this takes courage. Some examples:

- The courage to have others think you aren't cool, brave, or one of them.
- The courage to risk being left out of a group, a party, or an activity.
- The courage to give up some short-term pleasures because you recognize that it isn't right for you (or for someone else) in the long run.

3. A good comeback line

Saying "no" is a skill. How you choose to refuse something can leave you feeling good or bad, depending on how you pull it off. Most teens want to say "no" in a way that doesn't leave them feeling foolish. You'll feel much more comfortable saying "no" if you find your own style of doing it.

saying "no" with style

Remember the three leadership styles we discussed in Chapter 1? There are also three communication styles that go along with them. Any of them could be used to communicate the message "no", but one is a lot more effective than the others..

THE PASSIVE STYLE

This is also called the "doormat" style because it invites people to walk all over you. For example:

"Uh, I'm not sure. Maybe some other time."

A passive response reveals a lack of confidence, and that leaves the door open for more negative peer pressure.

THE AGGRESSIVE STYLE

This style is attacking or hostile. For example:

"What, you want me to drink and look as stupid as the rest of you? No thanks, loser."

This amount of force is really not necessary. You don't want to make an enemy for life. You simply want to let the other person know that you don't choose to behave in a negative way.

THE ASSERTIVE STYLE

This is the communication style that best fits our *Teens in Action* approach. It's both firm and friendly. For example:

"No, I don't want a beer. Do you have a soft drink?"

This approach enables you to stand up for yourself without insulting or injuring the other person. When you use the assertive approach to say "no," follow these guidelines:

GUIDELINES FOR USING THE ASSERTIVE APPROACH TO SAY "NO"

1. Make it clear that your answer is a confident "no."

When you're sure that your answer is "no," show your confidence with your words, tone of voice, and body language. No mixed messages allowed! Remember this checklist:.

- Be sure of your answer.
- Stay calm.
- Use a kind but firm tone of voice.
- Make direct eye contact.
- Don't defend your answer with reasons or excuses.

Repeat your "no" answer as many times as necessary., but never raise your voice or get upset: *"No, I want a soft drink." "No, I'd prefer a soft drink." "No thank you, I don't want a beer. Do you have a soft drink?"* Use this "broken record" technique until the other person takes you seriously.

2. If necessary, use a previous agreement or commitment.

You don't need to debate or defend your position, but it can be helpful to remind yourself about why you're committed to saying "no":

I've made a commitment to myself.

I have a lot of good things happening in my life I don't want to mess up.

I signed a "no-use agreement" with my family.

3. Know your reasons.

Again, this is more important for *you* to know than the other person. Think of why saying "no" is the right thing for you to do, or think of something you value more—a relationship, a goal, or your health.

My parents would be really upset.

I need to be in good shape for the track team.

I want a good school record so I can get a job or go to college.

ADDING A PERSONAL TOUCH

While some teens are comfortable using the assertive style exactly as it's suggested above, others like to mix it up a little by using a variation that better suits their personality, such as:

Add humor.

"No, thanks, I don't drink. I don't want to impair my reflexes. You never know when Chuck Norris might show up looking for a sidekick."

"No, thanks, I don't want to do Ecstasy. My brain is working fine just the way it is."

Reverse the pressure.

"No, thanks, I don't drink. You're welcome to join me— in not drinking, I mean."

"No, thanks, I don't do that stuff. It's not worth the risk, is it?"

Change the subject.

No, thanks, I'll take a soda though. Hey, have you seen Kevin around here?

Nah, but I would like to dance. You want to come?

Walk and talk.

Well, let's see. That makes three times you've offered me a drink and three times I've said no thanks. So, let me know when you want to talk about something else.

Look, I'm having fun without any drugs, or at least I would be if you'd stop asking me about it. So let's either change the subject or you stay here while I go over there.

These assertive techniques can be used in any pressure situation: not just the ones in which alcohol, tobacco, or other drugs are being offered, but also situations where you're pressured to fight, do something illegal like shoplifting or vandalism, have sex, or anything else that you want to avoid but feel the pressure to go along with.

Sexual pressure is a double whammy because it comes from both inside and out. Teens experience a tremendous surge in hormones, bringing with it a host of physical and emotional changes. Among other things, this makes you have sexual feelings. This is normal. The difficulty comes from the fact that teens feel physically ready to be sexually active before they're prepared to accept the consequences of sexual behavior. Teens hear a lot of conflicting messages about when to be sexually active. Most adults agree that teens should wait until they're adults or married. Movies, television shows, advertisements, and music encourage teens to do it now. As a result, many teens aren't sure what to think about sex because their feelings are so confusing: anticipation and pleasure on the one hand; fear, pain and remorse on the other.

To stand up against sexual pressure, you need decide what your values and goals are and stick by them. Always remember your reasons for saying "no." It helps a lot to have a parent or another trusted adult to talk to about sexuality. There's a lot more information about this in Chapter 5, so go back and read it if you haven't already.

PEER PRESSURE DEFENSE

If you're participating in the *Teens in Action* program, you'll be doing this activity with your group, but you can also do it on your own.

This exercise will give you some practice with your defenses against peer pressure Use your imagination to put yourself in each of the following pressure situations, first as a friend of the person being pressured, then as the person being pressured. Write a response you could use to convince a friend to say "no," then write a way to say "no" for yourself.

An example for each question is included. You can use it, modify it, or write your own. Just make sure your response feels comfortable to you.

#1. *"What's the matter, too chicken to fight?"*

Your friend asks a girl in his biology class to study with him for a test. It turns out this girl is going out with a guy at school who's known for jealousy and fighting. Later that day, the boyfriend confronts your friend in the hall, accusing him of flirting with his girlfriend. Within a short time the boyfriend is shouting insults and trying to goad your friend into a fight. You can tell your friend is angry and ready for a fight, too.

What could you say to convince your friend to resist the pressure to fight?

Example: *"It takes more guts and brains to walk away from a fight than to just start in on each other."*

Your response: _____

_____

_____

What is a good comeback line you could use if it were you?

Example: *"Look, we're both pretty mad right now, but fighting is just going to get us both suspended from school."*

Your response: _____

_____

_____

Continued on next page

#2. "Here, take a hit."

You and a good friend are hanging out with three or four others, and someone starts passing a joint around. Nobody says, "Come on, all the cool kids are doing it" or anything else meant to pressure you; the others just assume you'll do it. You have a chance to say something privately to your friend before the joint makes its around to the two of you.

What could you say to help your friend resist the unspoken but very real pressure to smoke marijuana?

Example: "*Just because they assume you're going to do it doesn't mean you have to. You can make your own decision.*"

Your response: _____

_____

What's a good comeback line you could use if it were you?

Example: *No thanks. I'm not into that.*

Your response: _____

_____

#3. "Come on. Everybody has sex."

A friend confides in you that the guy she went out with on Friday night used this line on her. This was their third date, and he thought they'd been together long enough to have sex. Your friend, however, thought otherwise. She was able to avoid the pressure, but the guy was so upset about it that she wonders if she should just give in next time.

What could you say to help your friend resist the pressure to have sex?

Example: "*Sometimes people exaggerate to convince you to give in to what they want. 'Everybody' is not having sex. Think about all the people we know who have not done it yet..*"

Your response: _____

_____

Continued on next page

What's a good comeback line you could use if it were you?

Example: *"Right. I guess I'm the last virgin on the planet. I don't think so."*

Your response: _____

_____

What if they come back with another line like, "*Well at least anyone who's halfway cool does it.*"

Example: *"Having sex is a lot of things, but it isn't a sign of being cool. I mean how much cool does it take to do it, anyway? I've seen pigs do it and they're not all that cool."*

Your response: _____

_____

What if he or she keeps pressuring you verbally and physically?

Example: *"If you keep pressuring me, I'm leaving."*

Your response: _____

_____

ABOUT BULLYING

Bullying is violence. Don't ever doubt it. And worse, bullying often leads to much more serious expressions of violence. We've all heard news stories of bullying victims who became suicide or homicide victims. We've also watched in horror as victims of bullying suddenly snapped and sought revenge on others, often on innocent students, in some of the worst school shootings in history. What rarely makes the headlines are the personal stories of thousands of teens on whom bullying leaves its mark every day. Fortunately, with awareness of bullying on the rise, schools are much more prepared to deal with it than they once were, and programs designed to prevent bullying are becoming more common. But many acts of bullying go unreported and continue where adults won't see it. Often teens are the only ones present. That's one reason it's so important for teens to take action against bullying.

WHAT IS BULLYING?

- Physical bullying: hitting, kicking, pushing, choking, punching

- Verbal bullying: threatening, teasing, starting rumors, hate speech

- Exclusion: Excluding others from group activities with the intention of making them feel bad. "You weren't invited to our party!" "No one wants to hang out with him;" "Don't be her friend."

- Internet bullying: Using social networking sites, texting, e-mail, blogging, and other online methods to attack and humiliate a victim, usually anonymously.

WHAT CAN YOU DO IF YOU'RE BEING BULLIED?

- Realize that you need support. Remember, there's strength in numbers. Ask your friends or others who think bullying is wrong to get involved.

- If the bullying is not severe, use your communication skills such as "I" messages and assertiveness skills to handle the problem.

- With more severe or ongoing bullying, talk with your parents, the school counselor, a teacher, or someone in the school administration. Work together and follow through to make sure the bullying stops.

- Don't be ashamed. It's not your fault you're bullied. Bullies will attack weaknesses and exaggerate them. We all have weaknesses, so don't get hung up on what they say.

WHAT CAN BYSTANDERS DO?

Most bullying takes place when other kids are around. A lot of these "bystanders" would like to help but don't know how. Here are some ideas:

- Walk away. This lets the bully know that what they're doing isn't funny or acceptable.

- Take a stand. Tell the bully that what he's doing is wrong. By saying, "That's not cool. Let's get going." or something similar, kids can stand up for each other. This may also give other bystanders the confidence to speak up or walk away.

- Reach out. Sometimes kids get picked on because they don't have any friends or anyone to stand up for them. When you befriend someone being bullied, bullies are less likely to pick on them. Friendship can also give them the support and confidence to stand up for themselves.

- Spread the word. When more kids stand up to bullies, they are less likely to continue their behavior.

- Get help. Some situations are too dangerous to handle alone. Get help from in-charge adults such as teachers, school counselors, coaches, and parents.

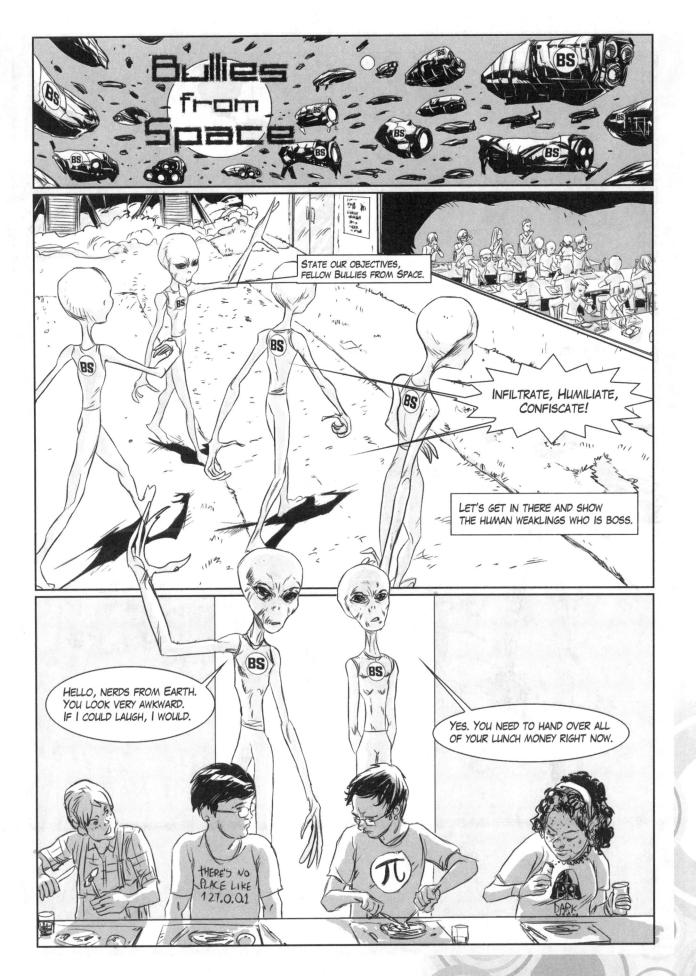

Written by Michael H. Popkin. Art by Juan Chavarriga

- Recognize that what you did was wrong. It may have felt harmless or even justified at the time, but it was neither. Ask yourself:

  What did I do?

  Why was it wrong?

  How did it hurt the other person?

  What was my goal?

  What's a better way to achieve that goal in the future?

- Apologize to the person you bullied and see what you can do to make amends for it.

- If you keep bullying despite knowing it's wrong, you need to seek help. Otherwise you're putting others and yourself in danger. As many as 60% of habitual bullies wind up in trouble with the law. You may need help with issues of anger or resentment before you'll be able to fully control your own behavior. A parent or school counselor can assist in finding a professional who can help you.

10 Risk-Prevention Strategies for TEENS

STRATEGY #9: IDENTIFY AND CONFRONT HIGH-RISK BEHAVIOR.

We said it before, and we'll say it again: It's YOUR life, and you have a right to choose how to live it. However, there are limits. None of us are totally free to do whatever we feel like because living with others requires that we have rules and laws that limit our freedom for the good of ourselves and others. This is the concept of "freedom within limits" that we discussed in Chapter 1, and it's the basis for life in a democratic society.

Another aspect of life in a society of equals is that we look out for each other. If I have your back and you have mine, then we both have a greater chance to succeed. Take a look at this tagline from an anti-DUI public service announcement that first appeared in the 1990s.

"Friends **don't** let friends **drive drunk**."

The message is two-fold: (1) Don't drive drunk; and (2) Don't let your friends drive drunk. It's not enough that you have the good sense not to drive while under the influence of alcohol (not to mention that for minors, just drinking is illegal); you also need to reach out and take action when you see a friend about to make a huge mistake like this. *Teens in Action* is about you having the initiative and skills to identify and confront all sorts of high-risk behavior in yourself and others. This can include anything from misusing sexuality to jumping off a roof on a skateboard to using drugs. And since we're focusing on drug use in this chapter, let's use that for our example.

identifying the problem: stages of drug use

When people get involved with alcohol or drugs, they typically go through four stages.

Stages of Drug and Alcohol Use

1 EXPERIMENTATION	2 SOCIAL USE	3 SEEKING	4 HABITUAL USE
Just "giving it a try." Teens usually begin this stage as a result of peer pressure or simple curiosity.	Teen begins using substances when available on a social basis, at parties and with friends, usually to fit in with the crowd.	Teen begins seeking drugs. This is the stage when addiction usually begins.	Use is no longer a choice; it has become an addiction.

Teens can go through all four stages in just a few months, or even faster with hard drugs like crack cocaine and heroin. But the progression towards drug addiction can be stopped at any of the four stages. It's not inevitable. However, the further a person progresses without help, the more difficult it is to stop. For teens who enter stage four, rehabilitation in a drug and alcohol treatment center is usually necessary. Preventing drug use altogether is still the best bet!

Since total prevention of risky behavior like drugs is not always possible, the next best thing is to intervene as early as possible—with yourself or a friend.

confronting the problem: the FLAG method

When someone is about to engage in a risky behavior, they usually ignore what they know of the possible negative consequences. Like the crew of the *Titanic*, they can't imagine that anything bad is going to happen to them. Some drugs—alcohol included—actually reduce a person's natural inhibitions against doing something dangerous or something that goes against their values. This is where it's important for a friend, parent, or other concerned person to step in and confront the person about his or her reckless behavior.

If you are the person doing the confronting, the FLAC Method is a good way to do it. The four steps of FLAC (Feelings, Limits, Alternatives, Consequences) can help you redirect your friend's behavior while demonstrating that you're on his or her side. For example:

Feelings: *I know you're feeling like you can drive right now,*

Limits: *but you're really wasted and in no shape to get behind the wheel.*

Alternatives: *I'll give you a ride home and we'll pick up your car tomorrow.*

Consequences: *This way you don't kill yourself or someone else.*

You can also use the FLAC Method to confront your friend about the larger problem when he's sobered up.

F *Hey, I'm really worried about you. You've been drinking a lot lately,*

L *and I'm worried you'll get hurt or addicted.*

A *How about having fun without the booze for a while?*

C *That would be a lot safer.*

You can also have this sort of conversation with yourself when you recognize that you're engaging in high-risk behavior and need to make a change.

F *OK, I've got to admit it to myself. I've been smoking pot because when I'm high, I don't have to think about what I'm going to do when I graduate from high school,*

L *but if I keep it up, I'm going to screw up my grades and not be able to graduate at all. Or I could get caught and arrested, and that would wreck my whole future.*

A *I'll quit smoking pot and use the extra time to get back in shape. I've always liked swimming, and going on weekend hikes will help me get my head straight.*

C *If I can't stop smoking pot this way, I'm going to have to ask somebody for help, because this is getting out of hand,*

threats of suicide and other acts of violence

An adult reading this book might wonder why we didn't just tell you to report the drinking incident in the previous example to an in-charge adult. While that might be a good thing to do, most teens will avoid bringing in an authority= because it may mean getting a friend in trouble. There are times, however, when you have to show the courage to involve adults, even if your friend will be angry with you. The two biggest examples of this are threats of suicide or of other acts of violence against oneself or others. Although a lot of teens will make threats against themselves or others without really intending to follow through, you should always take them seriously. The consequences are too dangerous to let happen because of a wrong assumption.

If you hear someone make a threat of this sort, tell an adult you trust. If you're depressed and thinking of suicide, it's time to get help. Again, tell a trusted adult or go to our resource page online for suggestions: www.ActiveParenting.com/TIA_Resources.

GANGS: SEPARATING FANTASY FROM REALITY

Gangs, it seems, are everywhere these days, even in suburban areas and small towns, and their members are from all classes and ethnicities, male and female alike. So there's a chance that you or your friends could be tempted to join a gang.

We can identify four main reasons why teens join gangs:

- To belong
- Desire for prestige
- Protection from bullies
- Thrill seeking

Understand that the greatest danger of gang culture is that it glorifies violence, criminal activity, and casual sex. Teens buy into the rebellious and thrilling part of gang life without considering the real consequences: a criminal record, imprisonment, debilitating injury, and even death—not only their own death, but also the death of family members and other innocent people.

How do you get through to a friend (or convince yourself) about the dangers of gang involvement when risk-taking is part of its appeal? Be persuasive by pointing out the differences between fantasy and reality. The chart below might give you some ideas.

TALKING ABOUT GANGS

FANTASY	REALITY
"Getting shot will make me seem tough."	Getting shot may kill you; or you could get "lucky" and live as a vegetable who has to be fed by your parents for the rest of your life.
"Being in a gang will protect me from bullies."	Being in a gang will make you the enemy of lots of people who didn't even know you before. You'll be much more likely to get hurt or killed than you were before, and you won't feel safe outside your own neighborhood.
"People will respect me if I'm in a gang."	What you get from being in a gang is fear, not respect. People will only treat you well because they have to, not because they really think you deserve it. And your fellow gang members will only respect you as long as you're willing to do what they want.
"I'll finally feel like I belong to a real family."	Real families don't force people to commit crimes to get respect and love; they accept and love you for who you are. Even if your family is having problems, being in a gang will not solve them—it will only make things worse.
"I'll make a lot of money."	Most gang members don't make much money. Those who do usually end up doing time. Plus, it's likely that you'll drop out of school to work for the gang or because of rivalry with other gangs. Getting your education is the key to making money, not joining a gang.

STRATEGY #10: **CALMLY MANAGE A CRISIS.**

We've made the point to emphasize that problems happen to all people and all families, and that through our handling of these problems we either grow stronger or resort to tactics that eventually make our lives much worse. Turning to drugs, sexuality, violence or any other escape from reality may make us feel better, but it creates bigger problems down the road. For example: a drug overdose, suicide attempt, pregnancy, or arrest. How you manage a crisis like this can make all the difference. Your priorities should be to:

STAY CALM. Don't blow up or give up. A crisis isn't the end of the world, just a larger, more pressing problem. Flying into a rage or throwing up your hands in despair may feel good, but neither will help you or anyone else deal with the situation.

GET HELP. You're not expected to handle a crisis by yourself, even if—*especially* if!—it's your problem. There are resources available in every community for every budget. Professionals are available immediately by phone (hot lines), while others are skilled at helping resolve problems after the immediate danger has passed. Some of these resources are listed on our online resource page (www.ActiveParenting.com/TIA_Resources). You can also call your doctor or a local mental health center, or find resources by searching your local yellow pages (www.therealyellowpages.com). With the right help, you can help yourself or someone you care about to recover from the crisis and even come out for the better.

MANAGE YOUR FEELINGS. Finally, work at not feeling guilty or not judging others for having a serious problem. It takes courage and skill to handle a problem rather than ignore it. Blaming yourself or others is going to make the situation worse, not better. If you've made mistakes, take responsibility for them, forgive yourself, make corrections, and move on. And show the same respect for others.

in summary

This brings us to the end of our Ten Risk-Prevention Strategies for Teens. Each of these strategies is a powerful tool that can help you take control of your life and move it in the direction that you choose. They'll also help to keep you safe and healthy, and even encourage you to help others stay safe and healthy. Keep a copy of the ten strategies on-hand for easy review.

TEN RISK-PREVENTION STRATEGIES FOR TEENS

1. Find positive role models.

2. Educate yourself about the risks.

3. Filter <u>out</u> negative influences and <u>in</u> positive ones.

4. Establish clear guidelines for behavior.

5. Make sure there's adult supervision.

6. Work with other teens and adults.

7. Find healthy opportunities for challenge.

8. Learn to resist peer pressure.

9. Identify and confront high-risk behavior.

10. Calmly manage a crisis.

FAMILY ENRICHMENT ACTIVITY: IN OUR FAMILY

Families have been the backbone of civilization for thousands of years. History has proven time after time that by forming small cooperative units, we can thrive. Families are a source of belonging, learning, and contributing for individuals and for society. To a large extent, the measure of any civilization rests on the strength of its families.

So whether you're part of a traditional Mom-and-Dad family, a stepfamily, a single-parent family, a same sex family, a foster family, or any other type, it's important for you to acknowledge and appreciate that you're part of a family unit. Participate in family activities, use phrases like "in our family," and help develop your own family traditions and rituals. **Find ways to belong, to learn, and to contribute. It doesn't take a lot of time, and it can really make a difference in how you feel and how your family thrives.** Give yourself the gift of roots by asking your parents to tell and retell the special stories of your family's history—stories that make your family unique.

GOALS FOR MOVING YOUR LIFE FORWARD

Perhaps the most difficult task for any teenager is to break away from parents and eventually return to them as a fellow adult. You still have time, so don't rush it! But it's not too early to start thinking about your goals for moving your life forward.

No matter how talented, smart, or good-looking you are, nothing great usually happens to you unless you set goals for yourself and then do the work necessary to reach those goals. Good things rarely happen to us by accident!

YOUR FUTURE IS NOT A MATTER OF CHANCE. IT'S A MATTER OF CHOICE!

Setting goals is like climbing a mountain. When we stand at the bottom of the mountain and look up towards the peak it seems impossibly far away. But when we really want to reach the top, and we can visualize ourselves standing on the peak, we become motivated to do whatever it takes to get to the top. Achieving your goals is accomplished the same way as climbing that mountain: step by step.

The beginning of the journey is always the most difficult and challenging part because you can't see your destination, and sometimes you can't even tell that you're making progress. As you take those first steps towards your goal, look for small successes to encourage and energize you, and soon you'll begin to see your goal more clearly. The closer you get to the top, the more excited you'll become, and finally one day you'll stand on the peak and enjoy your success.

Take a few minutes to complete the "You Can Do It!" goal-setting worksheet below as you think about some of the things that you want for yourself and others in the days and years to come. You can add to these, change them, or throw them out in the future. Because, after all, it's YOUR life.

I CAN DO IT!

REACHING MY PERSONAL GOALS

These are four of my personal goals for achieving success in my life, and the steps I need to take to achieve them.

SAMPLE GOAL:	Raise math grade from C to B
Action Step 1:	Study at home and school
Action Step 2:	Finish assignments
Action Step 3:	Get enough rest before a test

GOAL 1 (Short-term, in the next three to six months):

_____

Action Step 1: _____

Action Step 2: _____

Action Step 3: _____

Continued on next page

GOAL 2 (Medium-term, in the next year or two):

_____

Action Step 1: _____

Action Step 2: _____

Action Step 3: _____

GOAL 3 (Longer-term, in the next two to five years):

_____

Action Step 1: _____

Action Step 2: _____

Action Step 3: _____

GOAL 4 (Very long-term, in the next five to ten years):

_____

Action Step 1: _____

Action Step 2: _____

Action Step 3: _____

BON VOYAGE!

We have used the image of a ship at sea to describe the voyage you'll take as you leave the safe harbor of your family for ports unknown. We've spoken of the storms and icebergs you'll encounter, and how you can develop the kind of character you'll need as ballast to stay stable in spite of these threats. Yet, even with the skills you're developing to help prepare for a successful voyage, it takes courage to trust that you have what you need to make the journey.

We'll conclude with a poem that expresses our hope that you and your parents will have that necessary courage when the time comes to say "bon voyage."

Final Gifts: From Parent to Teen

Final Gifts: From Parent to Teen

Boats in the harbor are safe near shore
Far from the unknown sea,
But just as boats were made for more,
It's the same with you and me.

Those who would anchor themselves with a stone
In hopes of preventing a wreck,
Find that their fears are never undone
And the stone ends up weighting their necks.

We give to you a port called home
Where your ship is growing strong,
And when you need to harbor here,
You know that you belong.

We give to you the maps you'll need
That you may set the course
For places only you can choose,
So go without remorse,

Tilting your sails into the wind
With hope, and vision and courage,
I kiss you once, then touch your chin
And wish you bon voyage!

- Michael H. Popkin

TEEN ACTION REPORT

Write your responses to the following questions on a separate sheet of paper or in a journal.

about yourself

1. What are some of the most important things you've learned in *Teens in Action*?

   _____

   _____

   _____

   _____

2. What are your strongest communication skills? Which do you need to work on? Choose one communication skill per week to work on until you've practiced all of them. Use the following chart to track your progress.

COMMUNICATION SKILL	PLAN OF ACTION FOR PRACTICING	TIMELINE FOR PRACTICING
Example: Active listening	When my parents or siblings talk to me, I'll pay close attention to how well I'm listening.	January through June

about your family

1. What differences have you noticed in your family since you began using the skills in this guide (or since you began attending the *Teens in Action* program)?

2. What is one thing that you have learned to appreciate about each member of your family?

about your school

1. What peer pressure situations have you encountered recently? How did you respond? Use the following chart to record your experiences.

WHAT HAPPENED	MY RESPONSE

2. What are some ways that you can help others avoid risks associated with drugs, sexuality, and violence?

RESOURCES FOR TEENS

Want to become more informed about the challenges of teen life? This Teen's Guide is a great start for a broad understanding of the issues. For more specific and in-depth information, you'll need additional resources.

Visit www.ActiveParenting.com/TIA_Resources for a great list of resources just for teens.

If you liked this book and think it will benefit other teens, please help us spread the word.

ABOUT THE AUTHORS

Michael H. Popkin is the author of over twenty books and videos on parenting, character development, and life skills, including *Active Parenting Now* and *Active Parenting of Teens*. A frequent media guest, he has appeared on "The Oprah Winfrey Show," "Montel," PBS, CNN, and many others. He lives with his wife in Atlanta and misses his son, who is in college, and his daughter, who recently graduated from college.

Margaret J. "Peggy" Hendrickson is an educator and social worker with 25 years of experience in providing prevention services. Her credentials include a BA in English and psychology from the University of Michigan, an MA in education from Central Michigan University, and an MSW from Michigan State University. Ms. Hendrickson has designed, implemented, and evaluated a number of successful prevention and early intervention programs including the Families in Action curriculum. She currently divides her time between northern Michigan and southern Arizona, working as a consultant and grant writer for health and human service organizations.

Bring parents and teens together with a unique class

Active Parenting of Teens
third edition

FAMILIES TEENS IN ACTION™

NREPP
Included in SAMHSA's National Registry of Evidence-based Programs and Practices

When parents and adolescents learn together, they have a common language and skills for a smoother ride through the challenging teen years. *Active Parenting of Teens: Families in Action* is a video-based program imparting important communication, responsibility, conflict resolution, and risk-prevention skills in an age-appropriate way for both parents and kids. First parents meet in one room and teens in another; then they will come together at the end for a final activity to share what they've learned. Each class contains plenty of video, activities, and discussion to keep participants engaged.

BONUS - This program kit is actually 3 classes in 1! It includes the materials needed for a class of **parents** alone; a class of **teens** alone; and the class for **parents and teens together**.

THREE PROGRAMS IN ONE:

1 a class for parents: *Active Parenting of Teens*

2 a class for teens: *Teens in Action*

3 a class for parents & their teens together: the new *Active Parenting of Teens: Families in Action!*

For more details about this powerful 3-in-1 program kit, give us a call or go to www.ActiveParenting.com/FIA.

TEENS IN ACTION

Life skills for teens

Teens in Action is the updated edition of our popular program for teens and 'tweens alone. Featuring new video, high-energy games, and get-real discussion, this program is a friendly and fun way to reach out to kids ages 11-16. This kit makes it easy to teach important prevention & communication skills that they will use at school, at home, and in life.

Preview this program and see how it can help!

For more details, give us a call or go to www.ActiveParenting.com/TIA.

ACTIVE PARENTING PUBLISHERS | call: 800-825-0060 | go to: www.ActiveParenting.com/FIA | e-mail: cservice@activeparenting.com